Yda Addis's Travel Guide

With her father,

Alfred Shea Addis's,

Dispatches from late 19th century Arizona
and New Mexico Territories....

Yda H. Addis

Alfred Shea Addis

Editor: Sterling Saint James

Copyright: 2019, S. S. J. Trust

ISBN-

ISBN-

Parhelion House, Inc. Publisher
info@ParhelionHouse.com

Cover by Sterling Saint James

Graphics: Sterling Saint James

Victorian lines by Vecteezy

Introduction

"About five days ago a party of hunters came upon the bodies of seven men, near Ptacnik's mines, in the north-western section of Chihuahua, just beyond the Tarahumara country. From the fact that each of the bodies was pierced by arrows, some of which still remained in the wounds, and also that the heads of the victims had been badly crushed, the massacre from undoubtedly by the bloody Apache Indians, whose custom is to complete their deadly work in this manner."

The above travel dispatch appeared in the *Los Angeles Herald* on January 15, 1890, the writer was Yda Addis. Although she was a distinguished author of fiction, famous for her unpredictable, often chilling stories that first appeared in the San Francisco political journal *The Argonaut.* She was also a travel writer who overlooked the possible risks that lie in wait for her as a traveler in the American Southwest and Northern Mexico.

Most 19th century readers were unfamiliar with her travel dispatches; while her fictional stories have been collected and re-published recently; the following travel articles have only surfaced of late. These unvarnished views of her adventures could offend some present day readers due to her 19th century vocabulary; for instance her article entitled "Queer Mexicans" modernly could raise a quizzical brow. But if one considered the evolution of the meaning of queer from strange or peculiar to the 20th century connotation, some of her words were a voyage of their own. However, Yda Addis's 19th century title was not referring to humans.

Her travel tales begin in 1883 when she was asked to write a ten year historical account of Los Angeles, California, from when she and her family arrived in 1873. Later, as a well known author, she traveled throughout the American Southwest and Mexico where she gained inspiration for her fictional writing. Along the way she wrote travel literature. With views of people, places, social interactions, clothing, customs, and language—written more than one hundred twenty-five years ago, her travel tales could be described as visiting an entertaining antique shop. She did not try to offend, but merely described what she had seen, and experienced with the purpose to educate and to amuse the reader.

Her father Alfred Shea Addis (A. S. Addis), on the other hand, a well known itinerant photographer, and candid individual, also wrote travel dispatches for newspapers. His strong opinions and observations of the people and the politics he experienced while traveling throughout the American Southwest, currently some could consider his language bigoted or even racist. Unlike Yda Addis, A. S. Addis did insult, ridicule, and scold the politicians and the American Military. But in the late 19th century the manly use of language discussing politics, and society was different from the current "politically correct" point of view. The following example of A. S. Addis's travel writing was published in the *Evening Express* (Los Angeles, California) January 26, 1880:

"THE RED DEVILS

Are again at their favorite work of killing and robbing. Major Morrow, with the colored troops, is after them, but as the noble reds don't fear the Buffalo soldiers, as they call them, nobody will get "muchly" hurt. The universal opinion of those who live on the frontier is that colored troops are unfit for Indian service. Major Morrow, who is known by those who have been with him in action, to be a brave officer, has no chance whatever with the wily foe. For instance, a short time since, knowing himself to be near the foe, he gave the order to advance, and led off himself, when upon coming within sight of the reds, he turned to order an advance, and found that all his troops had found cover—he alone being exposed to fire; I imagine he felt as I did while traveling in Mexico. Some ninety persons thirsty being eighty miles in a desert, no water, no shelter to serve as refuge—nothing good worked out of it."

Major Albert Payson Morrow

Born: March 10, 1842, Montgomery Pennsylvania

Died: January 20, 1911, Colorado

Buried at Arlington National Cemetery.

During the Civil War captured three times, wounded three times, and promoted eight times.

Morrow participated in various expeditions against hostile Indians, including the 1876 Sioux Campaign and an 1878 campaign against the Ute Indians.

Mathew Brady, photographer

Above: Buffalo Soldiers of the 9th Cavalry; received the
worst horses & supplies from the military supply

Buffalo Soldier is a name the Native Americans bestowed upon the African-American soldiers as a testament to their valor in battle. For the Native Americans, the Buffalo is a scared animal, and they would not have given this name to the soldiers unless they were worthy adversaries in fighting.

In A.S. Addis's dispatch, he implied that the Buffalo Soldiers were frightened of the enemy, thus, ran and hid themselves. This may have been the case, but Addis's lack of experience with guerilla warfare most likely influenced his comments.

While A. S. Addis traveled to seek out unusual landscapes in the American Southwest and Northern Mexico, for the purpose to produce and to sell scenic views on cabinet cards, his travel writing was an unintended side job. When he arrived at a new town, after establishing a studio or gallery, he'd advertise in the local newspapers. Editors wanted news of what was going on in other parts of the country. An itinerant photographer was a good source of new information. From that he often was employed to send dispatches of the occurrences, the politics, and the cultural of the areas he ventured into.

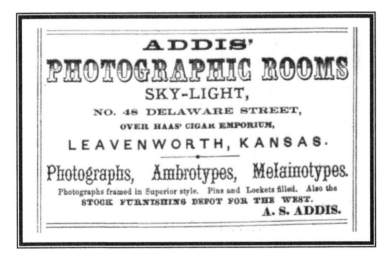

ADDIS'
PHOTOGRAPHIC ROOMS
SKY-LIGHT,
NO. 48 DELAWARE STREET,
OVER HAAS' CIGAR EMPORIUM,
LEAVENWORTH, KANSAS.

Photographs, Ambrotypes, Melainotypes.

Photographs framed in Superior style. Pins and Lockets filled. Also the STOCK FURNISHING DEPOT FOR THE WEST.
A. S. ADDIS.

A.S. Addis's newspaper publicity.

His daughter, in contrast, traveled separately from her father, but not foolishly. She did not go alone, but journeyed safely surrounded by a group of companions. For personal protection she carried within the folds of her skirt a Hopkins and Allen long gun. When the editors of the various journals, tabloids, and newspapers of which she was connected, discovered that she was going out of the country often they took advantage of the opportunity to employ her to write about what she discovered or experienced.

One expedition, in particular, she was hired by Charles Dudley Warner the editor of *Harper's Magazine* for an investigation concerning the manufacturing of "Mexican Lustred Pottery." She traveled to San Felipe of Torres Mochas located in the state of Guanajuato. Once she reached the capital city, she wrote "the distance from Guanaxuato is only some sixty-five miles, yet we were in the saddle six days, during four of which we made only the inevitable stops; this because of the broken character of the country, and the bad roads, which constrain the traveler to slow riding." The road lay in great part through a wild mountainous region, said to be infested with bandits.

As the daughter of a photographer, growing up in the family business, she learned the complicated method of taking and developing photographs. On this trip she brought along her photographic equipment. "We installed ourselves on the ground with infinite composure, and our time being limited, at once set up the camera that had traveled out from Guanaxuato upon the brawny shoulders of Pancho, the porter, whom we paid the extravagant sum of three reals (thirty- *

Charles Dudley Warner, essayist, novelist, editor, friend of Mark Twain with whom co-authored *The Gilded Age: A Tale of Today*.
Born: September 12, 1829—Plainfield, MA
Died: October 20, 1900—Hartford CT

seven and a half cents) per day "and find himself" for carrying this and some hundred pounds of other matters. It is certain that these Indians had never seen or heard of a photographic outfit, but they complied with a fair grace with the stereotyped request to "keep perfectly still, and do not move the least little bit until I tell you."

"The negatives secured, I proceeded to question them;" about the manufacturing of the unique product of lustred pottery.

Unknown products such as the lustred pottery were

novel, and drew curiosity. Likewise, the reading public desired to extend their knowledge of less known places such as Mexico, and especially the American Southwest.

Those areas held an increasing allure. Not only for their colorful landscapes of jagged mountains that formed curious silhouettes against the desert sunset; but also for the creatures who survived this arid, desolate place, such as the nocturnal venomous Diamond Back Rattlesnake, the Great Horned Owl, and the Coyote, who stalked, captured then ate most anything. And the indigenous people who lived from hunting, gathering, and farming. Through droughts, dry conditions, and high climate temperatures, life went on. Although desert life was unique, however, the most fascinating aspect of the area during the late 19th century was the mining.

It was when titillating stories began to appear in newspapers. At first locally, then nationally—finally stories appeared all over the world; reports of great veins of valuable ore discovered: it was a Bonanza! The opportunity of sudden vast wealth caught the attention of capitalists. And with that fresh money began flowing into the American Southwest and parts of Mexico. New mines opened up where men were needed to work the mines. Miners arrived and the investors followed. Mining camps needed services and businesses such as dry goods, blacksmithing, and housing. Boomtowns emerged where everyone made money.

Far and wide people were eager to know more about what was happening in the American Southwest and Northern Mexico. Newspapers fanned the flame and as they did their readership grew. More reporters were needed to go to the mining areas to observe, and to report back with descriptions of the events, the mining camps, and of the lifestyles. But few men and fewer women would travel into these wild and mostly untamed areas that held little protection from hostile natives.

The United States Military's presence was a scattering of troops even though the mining, businesses, and the population grew. But the indigenous people, among them the Navajo and the Apaches, often were not treated honestly by the Military—and A.S. Addis blamed the corrupt Generals and Indian Agents who stole promised supplies and attempted to encroach upon their reservations often rich with ore. The Indians retaliated as A.S. Addis reported in 1880:

"VICTORIO AND HIS BAND

Left the reservation and have been raiding ever since. Within a radius of 100 miles of this place has killed 111 persons, fearfully mutilating women and children after outraging them. And silly old granny Schurz wants to make peace with them. Out of such a dastardly Government that won't protect her people! Had such outrages been perpetrated on English subjects a whole nation of barbarians would have been annihilated. Even poor misruled Mexico, does better, offering $100 for every scalp of these demons. It costs Uncle Sam about one million dollars and two hundred lives for every Indian Killed. This is no exaggeration."

Above: Granny Schurz, A.S. Addis's term for the 13th U.S. Secretary of the Interior, Carl Schurz, who tried, like a kindly grandmother, to make friends with the Indians to have them assimilate. Later he reversed his position to dissimilation.
Source: National Portrait Gallery Smithsonian Institute

Above: Victorio, A.S. Addis referred to him as Vic.
Photo Source: Wikipedia

The Indians disputed their treatment, often attacking settlers. It was war for the Apache Geronimo, and the Chiricahua chief Victorio.

But the American Army was not enough against the numerous Apaches and their discontent. In a volatile and hostile atmosphere, travel on dirt roads that coursed through lonely desolate areas was dangerous. By stagecoach, horseback, or wagons, the trip was neither easy, nor safe. Not anyone could have the physical strength, the determined will and the courage to adventure into places where hostile

Indians, as Yda Addis expressed in 1890, left the dead "pierced by arrows, some of which still remained in the wounds, and also that the heads of the victims had been badly crushed, the massacre from undoubtedly by the bloody Apache Indians."

Both Yda Addis and her father Alfred Shea Addis through the following dispatches, letters, and articles have left a trail of travel adventures unlike any before. Perhaps the imagery they have created too strong for the history books, nevertheless, this travel guide tells a story like none other.

Contents

Yda Addis's Travel Guide

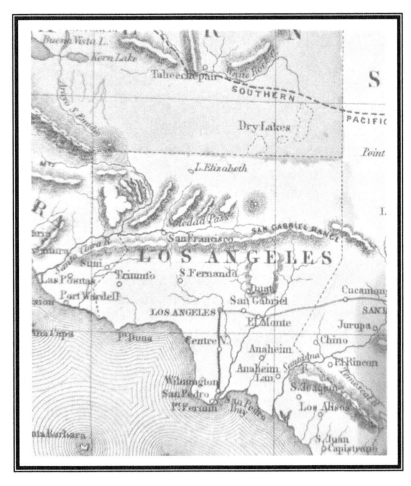

c. 1870: Map showing the route from San Pedro Bay to the City of Los Angeles.

A Gossiping Account of Los Angeles as it was Ten Years Ago

By Yda H. Addis

Appeared in the *Pomona Weekly Times*
Saturday March 17, 1883.

It was a muggy day in early October, 1872, that we landed at Wilmington, from the *Orizaba*—master, good Captain Johnson. The sea was so rough that the narrow steamer pitched almost beyond the probability of debarking; but then, as some of the sea-wise said; "The *Orizaba* would roll in a millpond."

We were closely packed—even the saloon had been spread full of beds—and we filled to overflowing the little "Los Angeles." Some one told about the then recent explosion, and the situation was full of ominous suggestions, so that we were more than glad to welcome the appearance of barrack, and the unsightly mud flats of Wilmington. As we had filled the steamer so we almost filled the train—then the only one in the county—with its shabby cars and very deliberate speed. I do not remember what Los Angeles people—then all strangers—were on board, except poor Mrs. Schumacher, who was killed by a train between here and San Francisco, three years ago. A good woman she was. There were also the two Misses B—, the youngest, with her nurse, bringing an invalid sister, who reached here, only to die.

Three or four hacks were at the depot at Commercial Street. On recommendation we went to the Pico House. It was in one of its periodical states on interregnum, and only rooms were to be had—no meals. My brother and I were used to free, active life out doors, with tropical surroundings; we chafed at confinement, and so set forth on explorations, pending settlement. Hand in hand, we two poor children, foreign of manner and speech—between us not half knowing English—tramped up into Sonora, perfectly fearless of its repulsive features and they were very dubious at that day; we stood with wide-open eyes of wonder and disgust, gazing at the Plaza, with its dry basin and grassless, treeless area. This was very unlike the Plazas of our knowledge, full of Verdure, fringed with lemon trees, comfortable with easy seats, lighted by night, and tempting with bands of martial music. Even the stiff, formal squares we had known in San Francisco were better than this parody of pleasure ground. And when we came back into the American quarter, it seemed little better, the shops were so small, their wares looked so inferior, energy appeared almost utterly wanting. In the old Abbott building—that low red brick opposite the Merced Theatre, and now occupied by "a milk depot," and the least changed of all that locality—we say a signboard with Dr. K. D. Wise for its legend, and straightway felt a little less forlorn at sight of a familiar name. We boldly invaded the office to learn if its tenant was indeed the physician whose tall form had been a landmark among the American residents of Mazatlan, and when we found him the same, we felt a little less strangers in a strange land.

The night we removed to the "Lafayette Hotel," now the "Cosmopolitan." [Full to overflowing was the "Bella Union," the "Clarenden," "St. Charles, "Grand Central.] Very picturesque was the old Lafayette, dark red, setting well back from the street behind a row of great pepper trees, and boasting a double veranda across its entire front. In front of the hotel were held the political meetings of the current Presidential campaign, and into these balconies poured the belle and beaux of the day, conspicuous in society at that time, I remember, were Messrs "Billy" Roe, and "Al" Gorden, who kept a stationery and furnishing shop in a low, narrow building between the "Bella Union" and Commercial Street. Both of these gay youths have since figured in the New York Police Docket, in notorious connections.

As the present year, that season was remarkable for a

lack of house room, and we found some difficulty in acquiring quarters, finally taking rooms in the Schumacher building, opposite the present Post-office, and next door to a little grocery store kept by John Schumacher. All the line of Spring Street, thence to First was occupied by small dwellings; the site of Larronde Block held a small frame house of one floor occupied by the Allen family. I believe the only business house then in that block—save Schumacher's—was the fruit store on the corner of Spring and First streets, still in existence. Across from Schumacher's was the boarding house of Mrs. B. L. Peel, where the best people lived, most of the professional men who were without homes here, and the house was a little social world in itself, warmed and lighted by Mrs. Peel lovely and amiable character.

(Continued next week)

_____

Saturday, March 24, 1883

Of course we were put to school immediately; my brother in charge of Miss Franky Scott, who taught the primary classes in the old house still in occupation on Spring and Second Street; [but which, by the way, is soon to be sold, for ever so many thousand dollars; report goes] and I was enrolled in the grade of Miss Eliza Bengough, then at the head of the Girls' Department. Miss Millett taught in the same building, and Misses Fisk, Bent, Howard and Madegan in outlying schools—the last named at Bath school, where Dr. T. H. Rose, the head of the Boys' Department, was just then meting out somewhat humorous, and certainly wholesome discipline to his troop of young barbarians—amongst them many debonair gentlemen whom one meets now in social contact, with more than a little inward amusement over his probable sensations if he knew how much of his schoolboy escapades one recalls. In those days Bath Street had claims to its name, the bathing house over the *zanja* were there, as well as the magnificent pepper trees before the schoolhouse door, relentlessly destroyed within the last year or so. Coming back to the Educational Department—in those days one Mr. Burnham was teacher of the negro school; and up to as late a day as Christmas of 1875, this schoolhouse—also the A. M. E. church—was the only building on those hills lying north of Hill Street, and west of Temple. But Temple Street at that time was un-thought of—a region of hillocks and barrancas, and to one who remembers "the lay of the land" then all those comfortable homes on the hill seem to be almost of faery origin. On "Telegraph Hill" as the newspaper reports of that day term it, the Central School was just finishing; Mr. Keysor the architect, and J. M. Riley the contractor.

I do not remember what denominations held religious services here then. Of course the church on the Plaza— dedicated by "Los Fieles de Esta Parroquia a la Reina de Los

Angeles"—was the field of Catholic devotions. The Cathedral was built long after. Saint Athanasius (of Alexandria) was then the rectorate of Rev. Mr. Gray. J. W. Stump was pastor of the M. E. church, which then occupied the low, large building— now a lodging home, on Church Lane, next door to the present church building. I do not remember who was the incumbent of the Congregationalist faith; that denomination retained the same building as of old, on New High Street, until very recently. Neither can I be sure about the existence of the Jewish synagogue then.

I believe three newspapers constituted the journalistic force of Los Angeles at that time. Tiffany & Co.—George A Tiffany, John Paynter, and Henry C. Austen were the firm— had the *Express*. The office then—and I think until some four years ago—occupied the north-west corner of Temple Block. J. C. Littlefield edited the paper, and a scrutiny of its columns on file shows communications and contributions quaint and odd, some of them over well-known names. When Mr. Littlefield became Public Librarian, he was succeeded by one Vincent Ryan, who had, in my modest opinion, the doubtful advantage of being the handsomest man ever seen in Los Angeles. He was so ill-advised as to publish certain articles unjustly reflecting upon some members of the Catholic clergy, and in consequence lost his position. I fancy it was at that time that J. J. Ayers assumed editorship of the *Express*.

Previously he had been associated with George W. Barter—suggestive same to old residential—on the *Star*, located just across Spring Street from the *Express*, in the old Stoermer building. Then Yarneil, Caystile and Brown were issuing the *Weekly Mirror*, from a small office in Temple Block. I do not know if *La Crónica* was living then. The *Herald* did not announce itself until the following year. All of the newspapers were very small, and all bore unmistakable signs that there were of the provinces provincial.

(Continued next week)

Saturday, March 31, 1883

At this period, J. R. Toberman was enjoying one of his frequent terms as Mayor. In the Town Council were Messrs. O'Melveny, Beaudry, Dennison, Macy, Workman, Campbell, Valdez, Teed, Ferguson, and Sablehie, R. M. Widney was District Judge, and Y. Sepulveda Probate and County Judge. Captain Geo. J. Clarke was Post-Master, but in December 1872, he was succeeded by H. J. W. Bent. The Post-Office was on Spring Street, in that portion of Temple Block between Iietman's and Lazarus' bookstores, and the arrangements inextensive and incommodious. The question of a Public Library was in agitation among progressive spirited citizens, and shortly afterward became a *fait accompli* with J. C. Littlefield as Librarian, occupying a portion of its present space in

Downey Block, with very modest appliances and shelf-stock. Having been too young at that time to take part in social matters, I have no distinct recollection of their condition then, But I do remember that entertainments of a general nature were very rare and of no high order. Traveling facilities were very discouraging, and few dramatic or musical companies were tempted to visit a town of twelve-thousand inhabitants, having—as it has not yet—so assembly hall of nearly adequate proportion. The skating rink on Court Street, between Main and Spring was the staple amendment and medals and fractured or dislocated hula alike were borne by a large percentage of the young people. Beyond this, the delights of an occasional concert or church festival, was about the sole diversion to be enjoyed by the young. We reached Los Angeles too late for the Fair of 1872, but the second annual Fair in 1873 was held in the rink building. At Agricultural Park, horses were entered for the races by Oscar Macy, George R. Butler, T. D. Mott, and L. J. Rose. It makes one fairly breathless, to look back in memory of those days, and range along the street with their wretched walks dimly lighted and dreary as they were. Days when little cottages dotted almost all the length of Spring and Main streets, save that space between Temple Block and the Pico House, and even there, the site of Baker Block was filed by the adobe dwelling of one floor, picturesque but not imposing, of Mrs. Sterns [Baker],

30

and opposite that was a row of dilapidated adobes not at all fair to see. The Cynoret buildings, Baker Block, the Cosmopolitan Hotel, the bank alongside it, Heinseh's Block, the Hellman and Mascarel property, the Ducommon, Allen, Central Union and the City of Paris, Mohr, the fine Schumacher buildings, Odd Fellows, Mc Donald, Larronde, Bernard, Cardona, the burnt district on Main, all these blocks, and a score of others in the space before mentioned, were missing from two—only two—of the principal streets. Imagination could cargo carry farther the comparison, architecturally, between Los Angles now and Los Angeles a decade ago—when Sixth Street was practically out of town. The busy bustling city of today, pared, horse-carred, electric lighted, linked with ringing rail to every import section, she has almost forgotten her old self. From the shoe-black, and the ubiquitous newsboy, up to her busy manufactories, she lacks almost no metropolitan feature. With her population almost doubled, her enterprise verified, her failures and mistakes retrieved, she looks back upon her old days with superior smile of affectionate pity.

Yda H. Addis.

Photo c.1875: View of Spring Street near Court Street; on the right is F. Adam Tailor; the top of the building is a sign "City of Paris."

Source: Los Angeles Water and Power Museum

Mexico-An Aforetime Angeleño in the "Sister Republic."

A Gondola Ride Down the Viga
In Company with Charles Dudley Warner—
Characteristic Scenery Along the Banks
—Tanneries and Calla Lilies

Special Correspondence of the Los Angeles Times

City of Mexico, July 14, 1886—

The City of Mexico offers to the sojourning foreigner at least one experience unique in value—a trip down the Viga—a survivor of that system of canal net work which so embarrassed the Conquistadores. It is an excursion I have often made, and ever with new and unfailing sensations of delight. In some sort uniting to the Characteristics of this country certain phases of Venetian life, this experience surprises and fascinates with a potent and irresistible charm. Perhaps the spell was in fullest force a few days since, when the conditions were particularly favorable—

the date was sacred to a saint of no particular importance in the calendar, but in high favor among the lower order as baptismal patron; therefore it was sure that merrymaking celebrants would abound. The day was the typical Mexican day, the perfection of weather, with an atmosphere of subdued and tempered brilliance; a soft wind was blowing; it gave the impression of coming perfumed-laden, despite the villainous emanation from the streets. And for companion, I think one might sift through one's acquaintance of many planets, and still find none so charming as Charles Dudley Warner. We had visited Chapultepec castle and palace in the forenoon, and had brought away an assortment of the aches and bruises that attend carriage exercise over these uneven thoroughfares. Therefore we contentedly resigned ourselves to the modest conveyance of a one-mule tram-car—I believe the only line in the city that runs a single car—and rumbled along smoothly enough to the embarcadero, unsightly, unsavory, but certainly picturesque. Huddled along the brink was a broken line of barges, their low, flat canopies lifted above the bank, and at our approach the boatmen swarmed forth and clustered around us, vaunting each the praises of his own particular craft, and his skill and strength in poling. They were not entirely unlike a group of donkey—boys in the Orient; what with their vociferous urgency, their wild gestures, their bare brown legs and arms, and attire for light marching

34

order. "The *chaparrito!*" we demanded, remembering a former trip under convoy of an eminent ex-jurist from California; "where is the boat that the licentiate Sepulveda hires?" The other men fell back, as the short, cask-shaped, smiling fellow marshaled us into his boat, blunt-ended like a lighter, and pushed into the slow stream; past the dugout canoes where an army of woman were scrubbing clothes; past a malodorous tannery; close by a house smothered in callas, roses and honeysuckle, whilst we could scarcely breathe the defiled, thick air. Once past the first bridge, we swung into a cleared stream, and the vista of beauty was opened. Straight before rippled the broad canal, here dark with reflections of the bordering cottonwoods and poplars, there brightly giving back the smile of an opaline sky. Now we glided past a ruined house, rich with the painting of time, looming against the light with all the dignity of desolation; then up-rose the tall, smoking chimneys of a busy factory, whose walls the water lapped. Mayhap next came a field, with yellowing grain, and "foolish poppies in among the corn;" and in the foreground, the sturdy figures of Indian women, with their dark, coarse skirts and wrapping *nipil*—their broad hats and rough bare feet, scurrying along with a little swinging trot trot gait, that seems to mince, but does devour the distance. Beyond a thicket of trees and brush on the left outspread an open space, and ah! the grandeur of it! A dark and massive outline, up-reaching like a faith, and resting there lightly as a cloud, firmly as conviction, in the majestic figure of a woman in repose, every curve of a perfect outline visible; we have seen Ixtaccihuatl, the White Woman. And beyond her, as if at reverent distance standing guard over her grand repose, the stately shape of Popocatapetl. A little further along, on the right hand, stands the statue of Guatemotzin, nephew of Moctezuma, and last of the Aztec princes dear, to readers of Leo Wallace's "Fair, God," *Cuaugtemotzin* his name inscribed on the great pedestal of his statue, which is not a statue, but a bust. On the lower ledges sat a man in company with a bottle of *tequila*: the fiery liquid had not consumed his native courtesy, for, seeing us studying the inscriptions, he civilly offered the information—superfluous as it happened—that they are identical—one side in Spanish, the other in Aztec.

We had left the narrow little side-benches of the boat, chintz-covered, in favor of a seat on our wraps on the floor, for the canopy is humbling to a man of stately height. The reason for its modest dimensions became apparent when we glided through the low, flat arches of the bridge. A hay barge had lately passed, and the rough stones had taken toll of its cargo in golden wisps that decked their austerity. A long boat glided near us; it was less pretentious than ours, and it held sixteen or twenty Mexicans of the artisan or petty shop-keeping class, out for a holiday—no doubt various of them named Epigmenio. Most of the women were pretty, with a quite Egyptian cast. The whole boat-load beamed with pleasure when we hailed them, to beg for their national hymn, and the musicians, having guitar, mandolin, and dulcimer, immediately played that stirring anthem, and followed it up with such airs as we called for. It may be said that this request, from an American, is tolerably sure passport to Mexican favor. They held their boat alongside ours as the two moved on, nor did we part company before reaching Santa Anita. To this little Indian town the boaters come to eat stewed duck, *tamales*, and the like piquant viands, the exceeding difficulty of whose digestion is sided by the drinking of unlimited and very excellent *pulque.* The narrow lanes of the village were clean swept and sprinkled, and the low thatched houses, dark and smoky, were hung with fresh green branches. Almost every would within the boundaries might have posed as an artist's model. Here was the scowling villain type, clad in the rich *charro* garb, resplendent in triple silver buttons, broad hat and jingling spurs; here stepped precocious-visaged little girls, whose entire costume was a single cotton garment and a wreath of enormous flaming poppies; squatting venders of food, and fruit, and flowers cut from vegetables, gaudily colored idlers of dubious aspect, and a complementary numerous detachment of the municipal police. Barelegged bronze fellows clustered about us, urging the hire of their canoes for "snaking" among the *chinampas*, or floating gardens, which are simply rectangular frock patches upraised by the process of piling up the rich deposits scooped out of the ditches running between. Penetrating among the gardens, beyond surveillance of the police, we were annoyed by the insistence of a canoe-man, over-zealous to acquire out shekels. It is unusual to meet with this unpleasant experience. As a rule, the utmost urgency of venders or guides can be overcome by a decided "No!" or, better yet, the lateral waving, in native fashion, of one's forefinger. But this fellow, unduly, exasperatingly pertinacious, at last declared that we were injuring the "made ground" by walking about. Then did the analytical subtlety of the trained observer assert its superior power. "Is this Mexican hospitality!" we demanded; "you are a disgrace to your nation—the first we have seen who makes the stranger unwelcome!" Then that barelegged, brutal fellow, with apparently, hardly an instinct above the curs snarling alongside, hung his head and skulked away, responsive to the rebuke, knowing that he had outraged the finest trait among his countrymen. There is something fine among a nation whose meanest answer the touch upon this chord.

The Indian boats were coming in as we swung around once more from Santa Anita; long, narrow, unstable dug-outs, loaded with the nicest precision of adjustment with great,

38

beautiful heaps of vegetables for the city markets. No little skill and sense of harmony the Indians display in the arrangement of their wares from the *chinampas*; piled in symmetrical compact masses of almost mathematical exactness, the boats rush swiftly and silently along, a stack of great radishes pressing their vivid carmine against the pale blush green cabbage, flanked by corded golden carrots or paler celery, with, atop of all, quantities of the abounding posies—perhaps the pink, crapy petals of fragrant Castillian roses, snowy heaps of white gillyflowers, crinkled deluges of enormous vari-colored poppies, or fragile sweet peas innumerable. And in the bow the Indian poler, clean-limbed, well proportioned, muscular; perhaps the whole ménage is there; the women in the stern, cooking over a brazier, the children and dog couched on refuse of the load, and everyone skilled in the art of trimming ship upon the narrow craft. Here, too, trailed along, with overlapping ends, great rafts of timber that gave the canal its name, for down this water avenue came all the wood used for building purposes, and as that material was chiefly confined to use for rafters, from "viga," a beam, the canal took its name. Thus, then, is spelled a charm, like unto none other in this land of mystery and glory. Here is limned on the heart a picture that will never fade away. So long as memory lingers, now and again in swift recurrence, with a beam of light upon water, with the vivid glow of a poppy from a field, with a vague, faint strain of music, once more will unroll itself the panorama of a drifting dream among broad, fair fields and curious ruins, guarded by the solemn mountains, lapped by the long ripple of waves that have molded history, steeped in the sweet, sensuous air of a land softer, more warmly living, more passionately fair, than that "where it seemed always afternoon."

Y. H. Addis   Calle Vergara, City of Mexico.

In Mexico
An Interesting Letter From Yda H. Addis.

A Whole Guide Book by Itself

How to Get There, and What to Do or Not to Do When You
are There
Valuable Information

Appeared in Los Angeles Sunday Times, September 26, 1886,
Page 3.
Special Correspondence of The Times
City of Mexico (Vergara No. 11), Sept. 10, 1886—

J have so many inquiries about the more practical phases of a trip to Mexico that I begin to think it desirable to give a chapter on instruction or information, for the benefit of prospective excursionists. First, the season: From April to November, or perhaps the earlier part of

October, is the rainy season in the valley of Mexico, and it is safe to count the afternoons being wet. Nevertheless, the facilities for transportation are so good, and the rains are so little disagreeable, that I would not hesitate to take the chances, especially if equipped with rubber shoes and coat. Apparel suitable for California spring or autumn should be worn on the plateau, with flannel underwear. If a visit to the coast be contemplated, summer clothes will be needed, and it is probable that the same would be required between Paso del Norte and Aguas Calientes, if the trip were made between May and November. A knowledge of Spanish is not absolutely essential for a trip hither, although the results would be pleasanter and more economical to a party some of whose members should know the language of the country. On the railroads, all the employees speak English; in fact, they are mostly Americans; and the Mexican Central people usually detail off someone at El Paso as cicerone to an excursion party of any considerable extent. By agreement between the Mexican Central and the Southern Pacific, a party ten or more could make the round trip between Los Angeles and the City of Mexico for $110, exclusive of Pullman fare, which would add about $30 more, and food. I would recommend, however, that hampers containing tinned meats, pickles, jellies, etc. Fruit and good bread are offered for sale at most of the stations, and milk, coffee or chocolate also may be had at a

42

reasonable price. Living is high in the city, room rent being the important item. A desirable room cannot be had for less than $18 or $20 per month. The best hotels are the Iturbide and San Carlos, situated in the same block and very central; the Café Anglais, across from the San Carlos diagonally, which catches considerable foreign patronage, but whose cuisine I regard as far from good; the Humboldt, usually patronized by American excursionists, which is inconveniently retired. At these hotels board and lodging can be had for from $2 to $3 per day. All are conducted on the European plan, so that lodgers who prefer can take their meals at the Concordia or the Bella Union, excellent restaurants, but dear, or at any other place they fancy. If sustenance and not style, be the desideratum, board can be had in the modest *fondas* as low as $15 per month—good board. There are other hotels, many of them, of various grades of comfort, some of them giving room and board as low as $1.25 per day; in this list if the Colon, where Joaquin Miller took up his abode, but I would not recommend it to people of tastes at all fastidious. For parties who intend to stay some months, there might be some advantage in renting empty rooms and buying furniture, which can be sold again at small loss, but for a brief sojourn it is better to hire furnished rooms. For my own part I would not feel at home elsewhere than at Vergara Street, No. 11, where I came immediately on arrival. The house is kept by Josefita

Dominguez, a Chihuahuense and its sanitary conditions are very favorable—the chief desideratum in this city of villainous drainage. It is but two doors from the National, the Principal theater, and one block from San Francisco, the main business street, in which are the Iturbide and San Carlos hotels. Within three blocks of us are the Alameda, the two American newspapers, Wells Fargo & Co., the telegraph offices of the Mexican Central and National Railroads, the Episcopalian, Methodist and Presbyterian Churches, book stores, money exchange, etc. We are in part of a building covering nearly a whole block, formerly a monastery, just across the street from the residence of the late widow—she having died within the fortnight—of General Santa Ana. The house is four-story on one side and three-story on the other three sides of the square. The upper floors are preferred; the nearer heaven one lodges here, the less likelihood is there of going thither suddenly. Only the lowest orders sleep on the ground floor, and, among them, the mortality is heavy, while it is not great among the better classes. We have a great central *patio*, or court, with flagged floor, set with handsome trees and plants in jars and tubs. A broad stone stairway of shallow stairs, in broken flights, railed with iron like the corridors, leads to the upper floors, where the walls are hung with hanging-baskets and orchids, and singing birds carol and parrots chatter in their cages. The first time Joaquin Miller came here to call on

44

me he was so enchanted with the picturesque *patio* that he would hardly go inside and ever after he insisted on drawing a rocker out, to sit in the corridor. He used to come, daily, Charles Dudley Warner, with his pale face, clear cut and delicate as an ivory carving, his bright blue eye, silvery hair and beard, and his light step, quick and sure as that of a lad of sixteen. The walls have heard many a bit of unwritten history that he told me of "H. H.," of Mark Twain, of the Dodges, of the author of the *Saxe Holm* stories, of Clarence King, and many another of the brainy brotherhood. Henry D. Lloyd and Prof. Henry A. Ward have been my guests, and Judge Sepulveda and his pretty wife, with their splendid baby, Carlos, used to seem to bring a bit of Los Angeles to me, before they went to Washington. Here came the Baroness Wilson, Spanish widow of an Englishman, her educational writings bringing her some $300 per month from the Mexican government, besides large subsidies from other entities. Here comes Altamirano, "the master," the Longfellow of Mexico; a perfect Indian in type, but of such wonderful power, when he speaks, that one forgets that he is less handsome than Hyperion. With his marvelous eloquence in exposition of Mexican literature, he sat here and held me spell-bound for two mortal hours last Sunday night, while the lightning outside was flashing green; and when my American neighbor came home he scolded me roundly for not having detained the poet until his return. "I believe you do it on purpose," he said, "you never have him come at the hours I am at my room, and you never keep him till I come in. You *know* I have wanted to see him again ever since that duel." For the two men were chosen *padrinos,* or seconds, on the opposite sides; in an affair of honor—which they prevented from coming to bloodshed—and Altamirano charmed, practical straightforward John K., as he charms everyone—the triumph of homilies.

Le Plongeon, the French archeologist, with his amiable young wife, lived here during their stay in Mexico, occupying the room that I do now.

Back to practicabilities. The terms here are about the same as at a hotel—say $50 to $60 per month, but one has the security of one's neighbors, for Josefita will take no guest who comes without recommendation or reference. The rooms are comfortably furnished and the board good. Everything is exquisitely clean, the food is of the best, and the *chile* and garlic—gastronomic prospective bane of Americans—are so little conspicuous that I have specially prepared dishes, the Mexican boarders objecting to the quantity of *chile* that I demand. The only stumbling block to American boarders here would be, probably, the question of breakfast, which consists of chocolate, or coffee and bread: but a beefsteak and eggs could be had on demand. For my own part, I would not know,

now, what to do with an American heavy breakfast. I can do any amount of sight-seeing on the strength of the morning chocolate, and certainly the lighter meal is vastly the more favorable to intellectual labor.

For a party knowing no Spanish, it would be desirable to hire a guide, which would entail an expense of $2 per diem; but this would not be absolutely necessary. Almost always some good-natured American can be found with leisure to tell what he knows to the pilgrim and stranger, whom he will "trot around" to the show places of the city. At least, the resident Americans will give information as to the lions and the best way to see them. Then the *Two Republics* prints a standing column of reference, or "tourist's' guide," which is very serviceable. All trips within walking distance should be made on foot, for the curious street scenes are the chief part of novelty. The markets should be seen by all means. That called the Volador is within half a block of the Zocalo, or main square, and it is probably the most ill-kept market in the republic, with its narrow alleyways, unsightly and unsavory, and its throngs of dirty, hustling Indian venders and carriers. Nevertheless, it is as interesting as can be, if one saw nothing else but the good nature on those ignorant faces—well, perhaps giving a glance at the greasy women in the butchers' stalls, who wear heavy necklaces of rudely pierced pearls, simply strung on thread, which are worth hundreds of dollars. Then there is an *alboleria*, where I triumphantly marshaled Prof. Ward, the naturalist, to see the festoons of vegetable sponges, and echinoderms, the great tortoise shells, the sword-fish blades, and mail of armadillos, and—tell it not in Gath!—bodies of polecats, split open like a chicken dressed for "smothering," and dried, beside a host of other queer and uncanny objects; the fat brown women of the shop sitting there, flanked by neatly assorted bundles of dried herbs, like a spider amidst the carcasses of his victims; all these objects are used for remedies. There is another large market, away at the lower side of the city, alongside the canal, the Merced, it is called. Not many Americans find their way thither, but it is even better worth seeing than the other, and should be visited late in the afternoon, when the Indian boats are coming in laden with vegetables from the *chinampas*, or floating gardens. Numerous smaller markets abound, some of them for specialties, as the bird market, the flower market alongside the cathedral, the old book stalls, the pottery plaza, and the junk shops. In the Zocalo a fine band plays on Tuesday, Thursday and Sunday nights, from 8 to 12 p.m., and in the Alameda on Sunday mornings until 1 p.m. To promenade in these two parks is always interesting, but especially at the hours specified, when one sees fine specimens of Mexicano *a Paseo*. On the other hand I find no enjoyment whatever in going to the Paseo de la Reforma, a

48

splendid boulevard about two miles long, at the end of which, in perspective, the hill and castle of Chapultepec loom up, with flare scenic effect. This boulevard is chosen for an early morning drive for health, and from 5 to 8 p.m., hundreds of carriages drive up and down it slowly and formally, their occupants being on show—a very stupid diversion. I may as well say, here, that the tourist finds himself woefully puzzled by the nomenclature of the streets, which change their name at every corner. For instance, the main business street running west from the Zocalo is First and Second streets of Plateros (the silversmith's), then it becomes first, second and third, and bridge, of San Francisco, then Avenida Juarez, Corpus Cristi, Calvario, Hospicio de Pobres, etc. But tablets with the names are placed on the walls at the street corners, and the policemen here are notably polite to strangers while if a foreigner be seen to stand helpless or uncertain for a few moments, the chances are ten to one that some Mexican gentleman will step up, and in very good English, offer to help him out of his difficulty.

In order to witness any religious celebrations or church functions, special visits must be made to the churches on appropriate days; for, since the laws of the Reform went into force, the departments of church and state have been widely distinct, and the latter rules the former with an iron hand, even to the regulations of bell-ringing. All street processions, the open transfer of the Host, and other public religious demonstrations are strictly forbidden. The churches, however, are always open to the investigative pilgrim, and the following named are those best worth seeing for pictures, or otherwise:

The Cathedral on the Plaza, whose first stone was laid in 1573, is a fine structure of mixed orders of architecture, which cost $2,000,000. It is built on the site of the great Aztec *tecali* or temple, destroyed by the Spaniards when they conquered the city in 1527. Faulty as is its interior arrangement and decoration, this is a grand edifice and it would repay days of study. In its chapel of San Felipe de Jesus, lies buried Agustin Yturbide, the first Emperor of Mexico, known as the Liberator; and under the altar of Los Reyes (the kings) repose the ashes of Hidalgo, the patriot priest, and Allende, Aldams, and Jiménez, his associates in the war for independence. Other churches worth seeing are the Sagrario, adjoining the Cathedral; San Cosme, San Hipólito, in front of whose site occurred the greatest slaughter of the Spaniards in the retreat of the *"Noche Triste,"* July 1, 1520; Nuestra Señora de Loreto del Carmen; San Antonio Abad, where the priests still exercise the old custom of blessing the animals; La Profesa, San Bernardo, and La Encarnación, perhaps the three finest in the city; and Nuestra Señora de los Angeles, whose strong point is a picture of the Virgin, discovered by a cacique named Isayoque, and miraculously preserved. These are the most interesting churches of the city historical or intrinsic attractions.

Very many churches and convents which were confiscated have been devoted to secular and private uses. For instance, this boarding house was part of the old monastery of Betlemitas, it was not a twentieth part of the whole convent, and yet, after months of residence here, I am still unacquainted with many of the quaint picturesque nooks and corners in it.

One most attractive place in the city is the National Library, which fills a noble building, once the Church of San Agustin. The institution is free to the public from 10 to 5. It contains some 160,000 volumes, many of which were taken from the libraries of the ancient monasteries when the Laws of Reform went into operation. Space forbids my beginning to describe the material attraction, even, of this resort. The bibliophile will find here treasures of ancient lore; and, also, a flair collection of current and standard works in Spanish, English, French and German. The management of the institution is very properly entrusted to Don José Maria Vigil, whose work is done *con amore* he being a careful student, and his own writings classic in Mexican literature.

The Academy of Fine Arts, usually called San Carlos, is open at stated hours that visitors may not interfere with the work of the pupils. The foundation of this art school dates back to 1779. It is curious to note the change of style in the really remarkable collection of pictures, from the almost exclusively religious subjects of the seventeenth and eighteenth centuries, through the phases imitative of the European schools, the stilted and conventional treatment, to the modern work, which strikes boldly into a new line, and takes for its motives truly characteristic themes and types of Mexico. Besides drawing and painting, etching, engraving and sculpture are taught to large and earnest classes.

In apartments on the north side of the National Palace is the National Museum, open every day except Saturday from 10 a.m. to 12 m. The gentlemen who were in charge of the Mexican exhibit at the New Orleans Exposition, now engaged in arranging the articles in the museum on a scientific system of classification, have very kindly given me the entry of the rooms during working hours, when they are closed to the general public. The museum is divided into two sections: Natural History and Antiquities, the former having but a small nucleus representative of the natural products of Mexico. Properly enough, most attention has been given to the collection and preservation of the antiquities, which might readily be destroyed, as very many have been already, through ignorance or vandalism, while many others have been carried abroad by foreign curiosity seekers. Here are carefully arranged collections of ancient pottery, whose style distinguishes the tribe of its origin, as the native races had clearly distinctive features in their various types of ceramic manufacture. Here are the war-drums of the Aztecs; picture writing, wonderful carvings in obsidian, and innumerable objects of domestic use or personal adornment, including exquisitely-worked ornaments in gold, the secret of whose welding can not be discovered or imitated by the most cunning workers of to-day. Here are mural carvings from Tlaxcala and other coast states, the figures of exquisite proportions; here in the great Stone of the Sun, wrongly called "Aztec Calendar Stone," which was, until recently, embedded in the western tower of the cathedral. Here is the huge idol of porphyritic basalt, about nine feet high, Huitzilopochtli, the war God, and principal idol of Tenoxtitlan, or aboriginal Mexico. Here is the Sacrificial Stone, which narrowly escaped being broken up into flags for paving. Here is the Indio Triste—a statue dug up in one of the main streets in 1828; here is the Goddess of Death, a most hideous squat figure, with superimposed eyes and teeth, and a tunic of interlaced, writhing serpents. Here are two gigantic stone heads of snakes, part of the ancient *cohuatepantli*, or snake wall. Here is a great serpent, coiled in pyramidal form—the serpent being almost the principal symbol in Mexican mythology. Here is Chac-Mool, or the God of Fire, exhumed in Yucatan by Le Plongeon, who still sheds tears of chagrin and wrath because the government would not allow him to carry it out of the country. Here is the shield of Montezuma II.; a picture of the Virgin of Guadalupe from the shrine of Atotoinlco, which was the standard raised by Hidalgo September 16, 1810; a chair, a gun, a cane, a stool, and a silken handkerchief that belonged to that patriot priest; the red damask standard carried by the Conquistadores; a portrait of Hernán Cortez; arms and armor of the days of the conquest; among the rest the breastplate of Pedro de Alvarado, Cortez' most indomitable captain, who saved his life when closely pursued by the maddened Aztecs by a flying leap across one of the canals; portraits of viceroys; the state coach of Maximillian, his portrait, and his silver-plated table service.

The National Palace should be inspected. It has a frontage of 675 feet on the main plaza, and in it are located the offices of the President, State, Treasury, War and Post-office departments, besides the Senate archives—comprised in fourteen large rooms—the general headquarters, astronomical and meteorological bureaus, museum, and two large barracks for soldiers. The Hall of the Ambassadors is a very large saloon, containing many portraits of historical personages.

The Chamber of Deputies in the old Yturbide Theatre; the Citadel; the Mint; the Customhouse; the School of Mines, which is magnificent, architecturally: the Medical College, in the old Inquisition building; the National pawnshop, founded in 1776, by Count de Regis, for the benefit of the poor; the Schools of Arts and Trades, for women and men; the asylums for the insane, the blind, and deaf-mutes, are well worth seeing; by all means, the cemetery of San Fernando, where sleep Juarez, Guerrero, Miramon, Zaragoza, Comonfort, and other heroes. This cemetery is closed to the public, but the keeper is kind enough to admit strangers, and he deserves a real—12½ cents—for his courtesy.

The American and English cemeteries lie just outside the city walls, accessible by horse cars. Admission is free to all the places I have named; in some cases, such as the asylums, application must be made for tickets of admission, and full inspection of the National Palace is permitted only on certain days of the week. In all cases the officials, as well as the attendants in charge, are models of courtesy, and desire to oblige. For instance, Charles Dudley Warner wished me to go with him to the castle of Chapultepec, which I had already visited, and I went with him to the palace to procure the card. The governor of the palace, who must sign the permit, was not in, and a gentleman at the office—a stranger to us, undertook to obtain the pass and send it to Mr. Warner at the Café Anglais. We two went about the city seeing other sights, and when we went to luncheon, we found that our unknown friend had called three times with the ticket, which he was afraid would not reach us if left. It provided too, for our going through the President's private apartments—a privilege by no means accorded to all Mexicans of high standing, even—and the man who did this was not a servant who could be tipped for his pains, but a gentleman.

In a future paper I will give directions for a short and inexpensive visits of interest close to the capital. Let me add that, notwithstanding all the denials made by Sedgwick and his backers, the cold, ghastly facts remain to prove that he did disgrace himself and his mission here. Indeed, the first reports fell short of the disgusting details, which would not bear printing. All the minutiae are known to the public, and, last Sunday, at the Teatro Principal, a play was given—to men only; surely that is significant—called "The Ham Sandwich,"— our envoy being playfully known her as "Sandwich." The interview reported in a leading Texas paper was faithful, being the account of a leading American merchant here, who visited Sedgwick the day after the affair, and to whom that unhappy man admitted the facts, weeping heartily over his shame. Then the Mexican, who felt that their reputation for hospitality was menaced by the results of the lark banded together to brazen it out for their unworthy guest, and suborned the hotel people. "What were you thinking of, H—, to sign that refutation!" said a leading American to the manager of the Yturbide Hotel. "Oh, that's what you fellows call diplomacy," was the reply. The Americans at the mass-meeting resolved not to expressions of condemnation, on the ground that *Mr. Sedgwick being a private citizen*, and *not* an accredited agent of the U.S. Government, his behavior was no concern of theirs! I am a good Democrat, but let us have truth, through parties go to pieces. An ignorant old squire in Louisiana appointed a young lawyer named K—, who was in the habit of making up the Squire's docket for him,—to defend a worthless and penniless fellow, up for horse stealing. The case was so clear against him that the young attorney for the defense, after the speech of the prosecution, said merely, "Your Honor, I will not review the case, but leave you to draw your inferences." To him the Squire replied: "All right, Mr. K., my spectacles are bad. Just you sit down and draw up my inferences for me." Which young K. did, acquitting his man. The inferences have been drawn in the case of Mr. Sedgwick.

Y. H. Addis

Another Spicy Letter from Lyda H. Addis

Notes of a Trip from Los Angeles to the City of Mexico via
El Paso—
Running the Customs Blockade—Etc.
The Los Angeles Times, 9 December 1886, page 6.

Dec. 2, 1886—[Special Correspondence of *The Times.*]
Vergara. No. 11. City of Mexico.

At the first blush it would appear that there can be very little variation or novelty in a trip by rail that one has made often before over the same ground. And yet I always find change enough to prevent utter bored ness. Returning from California to Mexico, however, little occurred, perhaps, of more than purely personal interest. I have, indeed, a recollection of a Dore-like scene when the train was delayed half an hour by a "hot box," and an amiable soul summoned me to see the picturesque effect. The "cotton waste," or whatever the stuff is that constitutes the packing of the axle, had been pulled out, and lay by the roadside, a long, blazing heap, while the figures of the trainmen, moving in silhouette shape in relief against the illumination, gave a weird, uncanny appearance to the scene.

At El Paso I learned that the political buffoon, Cutting, had gone East on [heaven save the mark!] lecturing tour with two kindred spirits. The capital of the enterprise was $500, advanced on ore from a mine owned or managed by a man whom I knew in New Mexico, he was then quite practical, business-like person, and certainly I never would have thought him possessed of so little "savvy" as was manifested by associating himself with the notorious international grievance. However, the El Paso folks declare that all the three are "tarred with the same stick," and predict their speedy return in a state of advanced impecuniosity.

Much has been said of the terrors of passing through the Mexican customhouse, but I am fain to avow that I have found these officials a most courteous, reasonable and obliging set of men, from whom many of their American prototypes might well take lessons. On the last occasion of passing, however, I felt all the terrors of conscious guilt, thanks to a lot of new goods in my luggage—commissions from friends who hankered after the low prices of American wares. However, I invigorated myself with the motto of the French philosopher, "Audacity forever!" and coolly walking

60

into the examining room took possession of the head inspector's chair while my effects were in limbo. A keen look at my unconcerned face seemed to satisfy the inspectors that I was a guileless lamb, who would not smuggle for wealth untold, and they passed my luggage wit a most perfunctory and formal examination. Just in front of me an old Mexican woman of the middle classes was eying her trunk, in the hands of two searchers. Several garments were disposes with artistic carelessness on top, and, these removed, there appeared a stratum of neatly folded white parcels, "What's all this?" demanded one of the men. "Only a little sheet rolled up, señor," the owner replied in a honeyed tone. "Just so," said the man, and he sighed the "little sheet," all around, poked it with his finger tentatively, and finally unrolled it with a sardonic grin, when out dropped six or eight yards of new goods. The same process brought to light similar finds from several bundles in succession, and at every disclosure the men would look up at me—sitting there beaming in my innocence! with the amiable smile of virtue condemning guilt, and shake their heads as who should say: "*Did you e-e-ever.*" At last the searcher gave up the task in dismay. "Now, honestly, my good woman," he said, "how much more have you there?" "Only three little dress patterns señor, I assure you, and of course a poor old woman like me would naturally buy where she finds cheapest." At that stage of affairs I saw that my inoffensive trunk was neatly corded up again, and I retired; but as the old lady was not on the train when we started, I inferred that her traps had confiscated. Only the night before a big sweep had been made from the luncheon hampers of a lot of swell American bankers and experts who coming down to look at a mine, and bringing a sort of branch Delmonico's with them, in the way of fancy viands and new dishes for camp use. I think, though, that this unusual severity may be explained by the fact that their Republican Highnesses, impatient at the delay at the custom-house, talked impudently to the officers, and the Mexicans stood on their rights in retaliation.

A gentleman on the train told me a cruel practice of the railroad people. Coming down to Chihuahua the train ran over a lot of cattle, some of which were only disabled, as for instance, one steer that had both his hind legs broken and sat up, looking about in agony. The narrator proposed to the trainmen to kill the living mutilated animals to put them out of their misery, but the suggestion was refused, as the railroad company having the right of way, do not have to pay for animals dying from injuries inflicted by the train, while to kill them outright by other means would entail payment for them. Where is the Mexican Mr. Bergh? Surely legislation is at fault in such a cruel decision.

The selfishness and ill-breeding shown by some people in traveling remind one of Joaquin Miller's story about a man who not only wanted to claim the whole world, but also wanted it painted.

Mining men and land speculators from the U.S.A. are thronging into Chihuahua at present, and I believe a great deal of money investment will be distributed from that point this winter, that is if the intending investors be not frozen out as the weather in Chihuahua is frightfully cold.

I have been in Mexico but a few hours, and up not yet acclimated, but "they say that if Minister Maming did get boiling drunk it was not in the disgraceful was Sedgwick did, but in the retirement of his own abode. I will give my impressions of the Minister later—have not met him yet. The American colony held a ball on Thanksgiving, for which were sold $1,500 worth of tickets, the proceeds going to the American Hospital fund.

Quite a large contingent of former Angeleños are along the line of the Mexican Central Railway. At El Paso are Francis Parker—who, by the way, has put money in his purse owning a fine three-story building on the principal street, the Vendome Hotel and other valuable property—Oscar Potter, E. B. Frink, S. H. Buchman, Dr. Townsley, and other gentleman: also, Lastania Abarta, the woman who killed Chico Forster. At Chihuahua are B. Stiebel, formerly a dealer on Main Street and the Addis family. At Aguascalientes I met Frank Pico and a young man named Buhr, from Los Angeles. In Mexico are

Judge Sepulveda and family, one of the DeCelis—Pastor, I think—at least two of the people in Wells, Fargo & Co.'s office, and a few ladies; beside, probably numerous other parties whom I do not know.

The mercury stands at 68 degrees this morning—a little cold for this valley of eternal spring: exquisite flowers are selling in the streets for a few cents a bunch, and oh! the fruit! Pomegranates, guavas, chirimoyas—the delicious custard apple, and a hundred other varieties charm the eye of one who has half starved on the poor supply of Chihuahua at this season. On the 12th instant falls the festival of Guadalupe, patron saint of Mexico, and I shall be able to witness the celebration at the villa of Guadalupe, the holiest shrine in the republic, the which I will dult chronicle and set forth for The Times. I will also send you an account of several important cities I have lately visited. Then *hasta lueguecito!*

Y. H. Addis.

Gran Teatro Nacional Ciudad de Mexico, Mexico

Life In Mexico

A Correspondent Discusses Mexican Usages, Social and Otherwise

Appeared in *The Argonaut* February 1887.

In view of the admirable natural adaptations for close amicable relations, commercial and social, between the United States and Mexico, it seems a deplorable thing that such intercourse should be retarded by ignorance of the actual conditions existing. Unhappily, such is the case. The Mexicans are more than fairly well informed as to American institutions; they understand the systems, commercial, judicial, and political, of their northern neighbors, and are even able to comprehend in some measure the complications of that more baffling anomaly, American society. But among Americans exists a most dense ignorance as to the conditions in Mexico; and that, too, among a class generally well informed, who can readily give the results of the last elections in the moon, or the features of the water taxation in the planet Jupiter, but who fancy a bravo lurks at every corner in Mexico to stab unsuspecting victims, or that the President is in the habit of stepping down from his chair, clad in feather robes, to levy little personal *prestamos*, for the reinforcement of a depleted treasury. The cause of this ignorance is not hard to find. Until very lately few Americans of the better class have come to Mexico; of those who come now, even of those established here, an extremely small proportion deal, except in the most formal terms of business, with other orders than the lowest or peon class. This is partly due to the difficulties of language, partly to American clannishness and arrogation of superiority, and largely to the exclusive spirit of the high-caste Mexicans, whose aristocratic instinct is unsurpassed the world over. Among the higher orders it is most difficult to gain access without due credentials, in the shape of social sponsors or letters of introduction. No matter how distinguished the foreigner, if he comes to Mexico un-provided with such social talisman he is left to himself. He may have his own reasons for desiring retirement and privacy, says the conservative Mexican spirit, or he may be an imposter or an adventurer, unable to command vouchers, or what not. The result is the same. Thus it has happened that many Americans, possessing both ability and impartiality of judgment, men thoroughly capable, in every sense, of representing the country fairly and accurately, have found themselves in a position inadequate for the necessary observation, and have kept silence, acknowledging their inability to grasp the subject, while flippant and un-conscientious scribblers have maligned Mexico grossly in their scribbled fabrications.

Being in contact, then, with only the lower orders, and not speaking the language of the country, what wonder that Americans know so little of the real Mexico? It is not easy to judge correctly the institutions of a land from the servants who attend in the hotel, or the men who sell one's parrots and lottery tickets in the streets.

It is not fair to judge Mexico by the standard of the United States, or of any other country whose history chronicles a moderately tranquil existence. This is a Caspar Hauser among lands—old in actual years of government, yet so retarded in development by long years of domination by a selfish, ignorant, and bigoted rule, that the country is still in its political infancy. By comparison, indeed, must the progress of the country be gauged, but that comparison must set the advancement, the enlightenment, the peace, the aspiration that obtain in Mexico to-day in contrast with the fanaticism, the still abject spirit of resignation, the ignorance, and the bloody struggles and tumultuous insecurity of two decades ago. Truly, the advancement has been marvelous. For the slow, tedious, and perilous travel of those days—on horseback, with plodding trains, or in racking diligence—the country is traversed now by railways replete with every comfort. The lawless gentry, who then took toll on every passenger, are virtually extinct. Life and property are as safe to-day in Mexico as in the United States. In lieu of the old, semi-barbaric isolation from the world, ignorance of the events of the day, and primitive institutions, almost every town in Mexico, of even average importance, to-day has a fast and effective mail service, postal delivery, and telephone and horse-car systems, while the telegraph brings constant record from the outside world. In every incorporated town, the local authorities, with all possible expedition, are establishing radical movements of sanitary reform, and planning wise improvements. The old picturesque mode of irrigation, by means of stone conduits or aqueducts, is giving way to underground piping. The question of sewage and drainage receives careful attention under the supervision of skillful engineers, both native and foreign. Bridges are being built, and high-roads planned, where ten years since the only means of progression was the slow and perilous route of mule-trail. Liberal concessions of lands are made to settlers, in some cases accompanied by subventions; to the founders of mills, factories, etc., the government offers generous protection, exemption from taxes, duties on imported machinery, etc., with often a considerable subsidy besides.

The financial position of Mexico is much improved, as may be seen from the late satisfactory adjustment of the English debt question. To this contribute many causes; the rapidly multiplying sources of revenue, as more and more of immense natural resources are made available, and the products yield their proceeds; a brave and patriotic spirit of patience and self-abnegation on the part of many government employees, in accepting reduced earnings, pending the replenishment of the national coffers; the energetic and decisive action of the people in striking down the bands that pilfered from the public coffers, to the enrichment of private estates; and more, perhaps, than all else, a cessation of the reckless policy which, with a mistaken foresight, sold its birthright for a mess of pottage, in prodigal, improvident barter to speculators who paid a mere song for lands and elements of exceeding value. Happily, this wholesome sacrifice of Mexico's great resources was checked before the harm done became irretrievable.

For the enlightenment and the advancement of the people much is being done. Among the higher and middle classes already the present growing generation is reaping the fruits of an improved system of education whose curriculum is liberal and practical, and available in its benefits for girls and boys alike. For the masses, the millions of ignorant, pitiable creatures whose whole existence is a mere animal being, and a continual bitter struggle for the mere sordid essential means of living—for these poor peasants, too, popular instruction is spreading its leaven, slowly indeed, but surely. The system of public schools, at least in the primary branches, is universal, and in many States rudimentary instruction is compulsory, even for the Indian peons. The normal school is not yet in operation, but the work of examining the qualifications of teachers, and their selection, is confined to men of intelligence and zeal, who realize the importance of putting the best material into the school-room. Another means to this end is one which might profitably be initiated in the United States, where the career of a teacher offers little hope of promotion, and none of support or position in the epoch of superannuation. In Mexico certain promotions and privileges accrue to the teacher, in proportion to his time of service, which also insures him, after a certain period, a fixed annuity. Such a policy imparts to the profession some value more than ephemeral, and corrects the cause for complaint, often made in connection with the public schools of the United States, that the teachers' rostrum is used merely as a convenience, a stepping-stone to other professions, as such inspiring no professional pride or zeal in its temporary occupant. The

72

originator of this policy in Mexico was, if my memory fails not, General Luis Mier y Terran, at present Governor of Oaxaca, the model State of Mexico. This capable and patriotic gentleman has established schools in every district of his State, paying for them from private funds when public moneys were unavailable, and in some instances providing the pupils with apparel needful for their decent appearance at the schools. There, in Oaxaca, too, were founded the beginnings of a noble institution, which shall, perhaps, do more that all else to civilize the yet uncivilized in Mexico, and purge away the canker eating into the blood of the country. There were founded the first of the State Industrial Schools of Arts and Trades, which shall enable the women of the masses to earn a sufficient livelihood by virtuous labor, and little by little purify them of their great social sins. The rulers realize that not by the gift of textbooks alone can the people be aided and redeemed. By the establishment of such institutions as that above named, and of hospitals and asylums for the blind, the deaf, the insane—for all classes of incapables who drag down the poor toilers who support them—by the organization of such practical means of benefit and relief, the government is aiding the bowed-down masses to stand upright under their burdens, and draw free breath before they essay to climb to a higher plane. The impatient foreigner makes much complaint at the slow movement of these reforms; but there is wisdom in the delay. The government of Mexico is acting the part of a guardian and guide to one who has long sat helpless, with bandaged legs. It is not enough that the subject be not forced to undue exertion; he must be even restrained, until the torpid members shall attain their due power. Thus it is that, for instance, mendicancy, while discouraged by the government in practice as well as theory, is not actually punished as in violation of the law, and thus is tolerated, from like motives, other features not in consonance with the highest enlightenment, pending the development of the people. In like manner, the press of Mexico, nominally free, is subject in reality to certain restrictions, needful under existing circumstances. Hence, also, the tolerant attitude of the authorities with reference to breaches by the clergy of provisions of the Reform Laws of 1857.

Not the least of foreign misapprehensions respecting Mexico is that regarding the influence of the Roman Catholic Church. The functions of church and state have been widely separated since the enactment of the aforesaid Laws of Reform, and it may even be said that their relations are severely strained. The major part of the church possessions have long been confiscated by government, and converted to public or private use, most of the public buildings being of such original belonging. It will, no doubt, be new to many American readers to know that monasteries and convents are unknown in Mexico; that to carry the Host in plain view through the streets is unlawful; that all processions or public celebrations of religious festivals outside church edifices are punishable by law; that in various districts the ringing of church bells is regulated to certain hours; that a teacher in public schools forfeits his position for the inculcation of religious creeds; that the clergy are prohibited from appearing in the streets clad in priestly garb; that the civil marriage service only is recognized as legal, and a woman married by the church ceremony without the civil form has no redress for desertion or ill-treatment, and no legal claim for support; in short, that she is not admitted to be a wife, nor her children legitimate offspring. Spiritualism has made some converts in Mexico, and Protestantism some; but so far as concerns the men in the middle and upper classes, an astonishingly large majority are free-thinkers. Freemasonry has many votaries, and that including the highest officials in the land. The intelligent, thinking men speak with the extreme of bitterness against Roman Catholicism, as having been the bane and curse of the country; nor is this acrimony of reaction surprising, in view of the fact that the expounders of that faith in Mexico were mostly priests of Spanish blood, devoted to their fatherland, and bent on contributing, by all means of ignorance and bigotry, to the continued abject dominion of Mexico by the cruel and selfish Spanish yoke. The influence of the clergy is still, of course, strong among the masses, but offset by the summary measures of the government; the feminine element, too, is extensively dominated by the church, but women in Mexico take so little part in active events or public affairs, that this second-hand influence is virtually *nil*.

That the constitution of Mexico is an admirably contrived document is conceded wherever its provisions are known. "But the laws are not enforced," says American carper. In reality the laws are here carried out more rigidly with less tedious delay, and with less immunity to criminals, than in the United States. Prompt and energetic measures are applied to meet the requirements of the times. A few weeks since, the press of the United States was full comment upon the summary execution of a Mexican who killed two women in a railway train. This procedure, which may be termed a legalized lynching, took place by virtue of a law known as the "Suspension of Guarantees Act." During the administration of Juarez, first President after the Empire, the extremely common occurrence of highway robbery, usually accompanied by violence, led to the passage of this act, to be in force for one year. For several administrations, its force was renewed from year to year by act of Congress just before its expiration, then it was let lapse. With the extension of railroad communication, the extended field of operations and the increased facilities for escape awakened the criminal element to renewed activity, and to meet the exigencies of the occasion the obsolete "Suspension of Guarantees Act" was revived, the immediate cause being an attempt to ditch and rob a train on the Mexican Central Railway. Since the passage of the act in the spring session of Congress of 1886, to other train robbery has been attempted in Mexico, and the records mark a notable decrease in the perpetration of other crimes to which this law is made applicable. Not a bad showing in opposition to the audacity with which the James gang defied the law and terrorized communities. All in all, the course of the judiciary in Mexico demonstrates much consistency, great impartiality, and a commendable moderation in avoiding the issues which would result from arbitrary extreme measures. For instance, in view of the uproar over the international grievance, Cutting, Americans resident in Mexico, regarding the country with impartial eye of the student, can tell of many complications averted by the discretion of the authorities here, by the quiet application of Article XXXIII, providing for the expulsion of pernicious foreigners.

In conclusion, it may be observed that these faulty and incomplete remarks, all in adequate and disproportionate to the pregnant theme, are not merely the expressions of independent individual opinion, but the result of intimate contact with, and study of, all classes of society in Mexico;

and the assertions herein are based on attentive reading of the Mexican press for many months, on reference from official reports to the heads of departments, and systematic study of the subjects in hand.

CITY OF MEXICO, February 5, 1887   Y.H. Addis.

Queer Mexicans

The Edible "Axolotl" and His Peculiar Flavor
A Venomous Scorpion
Centipedes Which are Almost Human
Strange Snake

By Yda Addis
Appeared in the *San Francisco Examiner*
(San Francisco, California) 7 August 1887, Page 9.
(all drawings by Yda Addis)

Did you ever see an *axolotl* (pronounced aholotay)? Did you ever handle a specimen of that anomalous batrachian?—if indeed we may call batrachian an animal which retains its gills in the adult stage of existence. Did you ever smell the *axolotl?* Did you ever—ah! now excursionist and "What I know about Mexico" expounder! Unless you are energetic and investigative, now, "Infidel, I have thee on the hip!"—did you ever *eat* him? Probably not! For the *axolotl* is not like the quail of the Far Field hunting grounds; he does not hop up and perch on the dashboard of the Viga-canal boats, begging to be devoured. And even if he were given to such antics, such is his un-poetic and non-appetizing appearance that methinks the average American tourist would on several occasions give him pause, ere acceding to the

THE AXOLOTL.

amiable proposition, unless instigated to acquiescence by devotion to the interest of science by the reckless, never-count-the-cost desire of a new sensation, or by the urgencies of a few day's subsistence on the fare of the railway eating-houses, en route to the only home of the *axolotl*, which his habitat it is in the valley lakes or lagoons of Chalco and Texcoco. What attentive student of Mexican history does not remember that "in the days of the conquest the *axolotl* was so abundant in the great lakes of the valley that it formed the staple of subsistence for Cortez and his followers," whilst they were building in the adjacent forests of Texcoco the brigantines with which to attack by water the Aztec city? But let none in consequence think that the Mexican President and his Cabinet sup daily on *axolotl* in these degenerate times. To realize completely how are the mighty fallen one must chase around as I have done, consenting yea! craving, seeking and imploring an opportunity to eat *axolotl*. None was to be had at the restaurants or *fondas,* and the people of the hotels and boarding-houses look at the giver of an order for this *platillo* as they might at one who should express a desire to dine off vaccine virus. The gentle hostelry-man usually agrees with the rest of the purveyors in letting the "crazy Americans" have their own way in all matters which involve a *quid pro quo*: but even thus much of complaisance does not extend to the degree of undergoing inconvenience or exertion for the sake of obtaining for the cranky visitors a thing they want, but in lieu of which they can be made take something else more readily accessible. The lower orders consume the sought-for beast by hundreds, for he is endowed with three attributes, which endear him to their unsophisticated hearts—he is cheap, he is not unpalatable, and he is nourishing—an order which must be reversed to meet the native idea of importance. But the *pelado* is a sly bird in some respects, and he retires into his haunts under too close inspection by foreign eyes. Thus it was that familiar as I was with the *barrios* where these classes hive and herd, no amount of prowling about the *bodegones* produced the *axolotl,* or if found, I failed to recognize him under his culinary disguise.

Bodegones, be it explained, are dens, dark, grimy hovels, cubbyholes under stairways and places of that ilk, where hideous old crones like witches cook up the food of the masses on sheet-iron plates and clay *comates* over braziers.

A BODEGON.

The messes are quite unearthly in appearance and thoroughly Plutonian as to order, and the hissing, spluttering and popping they emit is none the more reassuring to sensitive nerves. Yet all of these investigated I. No *axolotl*. My first actual introduction to the creature was by means of the olfactories. Seating myself one day in a hackney coach to accompany Henry A. Ward, the naturalist, down the Viga, that indefatigable traveler and genial companion, mildly requested me to take the windward side, "as the *axolotl* smell less loudly over there." And behold! He had a five-gallon holder full of them baptized in alcohol in a state of great debility quite overpowered by the aroma of "the bugs." And our errand that very moment was for more. Professor Ward having set his heart on carrying away more than a thousand. He did it, too, by connivance with a retired bull-fighter who keeps a saloon on the Viga, who in his turn got them from the boatman coming down from the lakes. Now, the condition down in which these particular specimens were present was less attractive even than is their usual wont, and their gastronomical possibilities remained an unknown quantity until my longings and misadventures were one day lugubriously related at the home of a Mexican scientist, a member of the Geographical Exploring Commission. "Now, have no farther care, for you shall eat *axolotl*," declared the hosts, and the next day a barefoot serving woman conveyed to my quarter what strongly resembled eight little skinned snakes floating in a pea-green gravy of Chile peppers.

There was an uncanny attachment or head and a little sharp fin-like claws. The sight was not one to rejoice a well-bred stomach, but I shut the eyes of the imagination and like the woman in the "poem," "I boldly waded in." And really the thing was good. It was a little like chicken, and it was a bit like fish and it was a trifle like frog, and on the whole it was savory, a slight flatness of flavor being corrected by the piquant chile.

Now as to the characteristics of Señor Axolotl; he is a peculiar-looking citizen from eight to fourteen inches long. He is known to naturalists as Siredon, with, if I mistake not, the

Mexicans tacked on as a distinctive feature. He is not a gigantic tadpole, nor yet is he a lizard, although he partakes of the attributes of both. His pollywog-shaped body is elongated, so that he has quite a respectable show of tail to serve as a rudder in swimming, while the existence of feet, those of adapted, while the existence of feet, those of the front with four toes, of the other pair with five, would seem to indicate that he is amphibious, and retires to terra firma on occasion, although he is popularly considered aquatic, thanks to the rudimentary state of his lungs. His head is flat and wicked looking, his snout box-shaped or truncated, and eyes have a peculiar set. His sides are marked by several small furrows and one important lateral line from the gills to the tail. Near the back of the head commences a thin membrane, upright like the dorsal fin of a fish, which gradually rises to the height of about an inch and a half at the middle of the tail, which it rounds, extending beneath to the vent. He is of a dirty dark hue, much like the catfish, whose skin his own resembles. The Scientific Commission before named became possessed of an albino—a white *axolotl,* which its vendor declared had rained down—and it was kept in a tank at the museum at Tacubaya, where it thrived, until it was clawed out by a pet *tejon* (raccoon) with tastes similar to mine.

The field month for this game bird is June, when immense numbers are caught in the lagoons Chalco and

Texcoco, 8,000 feet higher than the sea level where the water is never colder than 60 degrees Fahrenheit. It is much to be deplored that the social, domestic and business habits of this animal have not been studied more closely. It is probable, in the extreme, that he if gifted with many engaging habits and graces which would endear him to the world at large. I have a theory concerning him, for whose discovery I claim a copyright. At certain seasons wild ducks by the thousands are slaughtered around these same lagoons, and it is quite the fashion to be poled down the canal barges, to eat duck cooked in the fashion, at Santa Anita, Ixtacalco and other similar villages on the banks of the canal. It is my firm conviction that this is but an allotropic form of devouring the *axolotl*, which, according to my theory, alters his name and form, as bobolink becomes "reedbird" and other species.

Among the lower classes of Mexicans the *axolotl* is deemed a sovereign remedy in cases of jaundice and rickets, the meat being given to the patient as nourishing food, while he is bathed in the water in which the same had been boiled.

The Vinagron

If I were asked what if the chief bugbear of the Americas residents in Chihuahua, I would unhesitatingly and most veraciously reply, "The vinagron!" From the day of my arrival I heard blood-curdling horrors of this malignant and venomous animal, for whose bites or pinch, for it is

The Vinagron.

demonstrated that he does his biting with his claws, there is said to be no known cure. One American lady was fond of relating in tragic tones the account of a colony of vinagrones that had taken up their abode beneath her refrigerator forming processions into her dining-room, new relays taking the place of her slain fast as killed. There is not question that the mate of the slaughtered vinagron appears promptly on the scene, whether to seek on to avenge its comrade. I made a special *encargo*, or commission, to a party of masons and diggers, men working in places apt to be tenanted by the beasties, offering to reward them for such specimens as they should bring, and all I ever succeeded in obtaining from them was one miserable creature, too small to see what he really looked like, and at that with his tail cut off by the chop of a trowel. This was an irreparable and most serious drawback, as one of the most engaging attributes of the vinagron is the thoroughly feline manner in which, when excited, he waves and lashes his long wiry tail, it was months after this unsatisfactory find that one of the ladies of the family rushed in from the kitchen, pallid and trembling, crying "A vinagron! an awful great big vinagron!" and the company assembled moved on the enemy's works. In good truth there was no mistake this time. He squatted in the angle of floor and wall— a big brown fellow, a good four inches long, without counting the tail, and he looked at us wickedly and vindictively, with much the expression of a tiger crouching for its spring. The disparity in numbers implied him to make off, however, and his swift movement had almost carried him under cover when I persuaded him to tarry by the application of an American broom. Neither chloroform nor ether was forthcoming, and instead, he was liberally dosed with strong amounts. As the stream struck him he squirmed and wriggled, and then ascended from his ugly body, rising a yard high or more, clouds of dense white fume, much like stream in appearance, that filled the room with its strong pungent odor, like that of the vinegar slightly turned, from which he takes his common name in Spanish. The intensity of the smell can be imagined, when it is remembered that it overcame the odor of strong ammonia. Then all the joints in the animal's shell or armor cracked open and showed the delicate, tender-looking flesh within, pink-tinted like that of a shrimp. Whilst we were examining it the creature, wonderfully tenacious of life, began to revive, and his resuscitation was so rapid that it was all we could do to shunt him off in time into a wide-mouthed bottle full of *aguardiente*, where reposed in peace the smaller specimen aforementioned and two overgrown centipedes, of which more anon.

The scientific term for the *vinagron* is *Thelyphonida gigantus*, and in plain English he is known as the "whip scorpion," from the cited demonstrations with his caudal appendage. The gentleman is nocturnal in his habits, lurking in dampish places, under wood, stones, etc., until twilight, when he sallies forth for food. He is very active and pugnacious and can be drawn from his lair by means of a rag or paper waved before the entrance, when he rushes forth to battle. The more spirited children of Chihuahua improvise little simulated bullfights in this manner.

The lower classes there are abjectly afraid of the venom of our unhandsome friend, but I known of but one well authenticated case of its injuring a human. In that instance the effect was certainly disastrous; a party of road-makers went into camp at night, and as soon as rolled in his blankets, one of them screamed with pain. On examination a vinagron was found clinging to his back by the chelicerae. These large, prehensile, jaw-like claws are a development of the antennae, whose own function as organs of touch is in turn performed by the front pair of legs, which are long and flexible. The

88

victim on this occasion, which took place years ago, did not die, but he has been a hopeless invalid ever since, though he was a robust man when injured.

There seems to be a certain compensating sluggishness of disposition toward attack, at least in Chihuahua, for I have known several cases where the animal has been picked up by mistake, or found in garments hastily donned, with no injury beyond a scare. The vinagron is common in at least one section of the United States, being abundant in Florida, where he is known as the "mule-killer," and many valuable animals are annually lost through his attentions, a mule or a horse seldom surviving more than an hour after the attack.

A Centipede Incident.

In one of the centipedes above mentioned I witnessed an instance of animal affection, not to say heroic courage and devotion, not always displayed by frail humanity. One night an American lady living in Chihuahua, while passing through the court of an ancient mansion, set up the cry of "Centipede!" and on lights being brought it was discovered that she had stepped upon and partly crushed a large one.

We were looking at the repulsive articulate some seven inches long, when another, yet larger, issued from under a stone slab near by, and, running to its mate, grasped that wounded partner firmly and made off, dragging, the other. We blocked up the crack from which it had come, when it loosened its hold on its partner and ran hither and thither, seeking with touching solicitude a place of refuge. The mouth of the bottle being held near, it manifested unmistakable satisfaction, and returning to its mate, seized and dragged it into the bottle. I confess to feeling myself a party to a cowardly and cruel deed when *aguardiente* was poured over them.

The Maqueche

It is not long since many newspaper paragraphs were current concerning a pretty beetle which ladies were wearing on the corsage, where it crawled at will, held by a tiny golden chain. This is the *maqueche,* an *apterous coleopter,* a native of Yucatan. It is of various colors, but these of gilded hue are thus by artificial process, which results as fatally as the case of the boy gilded to represent a cherub in a papal coronation pageant. The upper part of the body is as hard as tortoise shell. They are perfectly inoffensive; they do not bite or sting, have no order, and do not deface or stain the most delicate

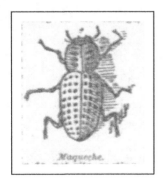

Maqueche.

His Harness.

fabric. The adjustment of their golden harness is a nice operation, the metal being soldered on them—a girdle about the waist between thorax and abdomen, to which, above and below, is joined a slender band, passing over the posterior portion of the body longitudinally, while a tiny chain is attached by a little staple, and terminates in a hook or pin to fasten in the bodice. By many Mexicans they are regarded as amulets or mascots, and they are usually highly prized by foreigners when obtainable. They had several of them. One is worn by Juan de Dios Peza, most polished of the Mexican poets, who is very fond of the little creatures, carrying it always with him, inside his coat, upon his waistcoat. Señor Peza, in the interest of his pet, made a discovery of infinite value to the *Maqueche.* The ladies who owned these insects had attempted to maintain them on sugar and water, but they always perished in a brief while. Señor Peza learned by experiment that their natural aliment is derived from decayed wood, and he has been able to keep his favorite nearly a year, and it is thriving.

A Legend of the Cencoatl

A propos to that instinct in the lower animals which at times closely approaches the reasoning faculty, the commoner classes of Mexicans have a curious belief regarding a certain snake. This serpent, called *cencoatl,* is a harmless species; I think it is called "house-snake" of "chicken-snake" in English.

These people aver that if ever it finds a nursing mother asleep it robs her of the milk that should nourish her infant, cheating the babe, if that innocent victim hungers and enters a protest, by deftly introducing the point of its tail in the mouth of the babe!

Y. H. Addis

Queretaro.

Interesting Letter from Miss Yda H. Addis.

Historical Occurrences

Scenes In and About a Renowned City.

The Tragic Imperial Drama.

Appeared in *The Los Angeles Herald*,
December 15, 1887

I have just returned from a visit to Queretaro—historic Queretaro stage where was played the last act of the tragic Imperial drama of the French Intervention in Mexico. It is not a place designed by nature for a battle-ground; nor does the tranquil, smiling landscape wear the scars of the dreadful experience through which the city has passed. One leaves the station of the Mexican Central, and rumbles up town in the ubiquitous tramcar—in thin particular instance, by the way, the fare is 10 cents, which is an outrage, 6¼ cents being the rule all over Mexico, save at Guanaxnato, where the distance is measured into stations, with charges accordingly. There is a sort of stameta, whose praises are chanted loudly by the misguided authors of certain guide-books, and from it one passes into the streets, which are narrow, mechanized, and certainly empty and sleepy enough for the thoroughfares of some littlie mountain village, rather than a capital city of 35,000 souls, on the line of the chief railway in Mexico. The markets are dull—indeed, it might almost be said that the whole streets are markets from the numerous huckster stalls spread out along the sidewalks. The fruit supply is excellent and the prices very reasonable. Oranges, *grenaditas*, a peculiar oval fruit the size of a goose-egg, the succulent *aguacate*, or alligator pear, peaches, pears, figs and quinces, the delicious *chirimoya* or custard-apple, both of which make superlative jelly, pecans and English walnuts—such are a few of the gastronomic attractions of Queretaro. Almost all of them may be had in crystallized form, for this is a great city for *dulces*. The confections of Queretaro are widely known through out the Republic, and they command relatively high prices, though they are cheap enough, in all conscience Exquisite in flavor and unadulterated, I regard this article as superior to the finest of French candies, and one day some other genius will discover the fact and will make a lot of money by its export. I must not forget to say that the Mexicans are particularly fond of the Queretaro conserve,

94

made of sweet potato—the which is used in its entirety, barring the jacket. The *palacio*, or state building, is a commodious though unpretentious structure, in where it does indeed "seem always afternoon," if one may venture on that threadbare quotation to express the conventual stillness within the edifice. The only thing in palacio worth seeing—and the only sensationally—is the casket in which the body of Maximilian lay for some days after the execution, and which is still stained with his blood. I may as well admit that I did not see it. My *ciceron*, a Spanish gentleman of high position and fine attainments, had made the needful arrangements with Governor Cosio, but when we arrived the Governor had been summoned to an unexpected council, and the officials about the place, after some skirmishing, were obliged to state that the porter had carried away the keys of the chamber where the casket lay. Señor de C—was simply furious, "*Cosas de Mexico*, in deed!" he raged, when I tried to soothe him; "nowhere else in the world could such things happen! I say nothing of the failure to comply with the Governor's order— nowhere but in Mexico would the door porter be entrusted with the keys that alone protect a relic of historic interest. What guarantee have they that the rogue will not sell it to the first person who offers him fifty dollars for leave to steal it?" I might have criticized more freely had I not suspected that, my own vandalism was to blame in this way. The porter's daughter was housemaid to the family I was visiting, and I think she heard my remark to sweet Pepita Valencia, that I proposed to try how far a bit of silver suasion would go towards obtaining a sizable splinter from the casket. This being repeated to Master Porter, he no doubt reasoned that I would not be so audacious as to attempt briery in the presence of officials and bigwigs, and so removed himself so that I might later seek a more fitting opportunity. However, that was my last day in Queretaro, so his shrewdness was at fault. To go backward in the career of Maximilian: On June 19, 1867, he was shot, in accordance with the sentence of a court-martial, on a crest or eminence known as El Cerro de las Compañas, about a league west of the city As everybody knows, the press has lately been much occupied with the question as to whether General Miguel Lopes did or did not betray the unfortunate young Emperor. In Queretaro the opinion prevails that Lopez is that basest of traitors, a man who adds insult to injury by seeking to blacken the character of his victim. Maximilian had the gift of endearing himself to those about him, and solid business men of Queretaro have tears in their eyes when they speak of his winning nature and tell how, to the very last, he was in deed and in word a brave, loyal, honorable gentleman, incapable of double-dealing. At the Cerro, where, by the way, were the fortifications of the Imperial army, three simple granite columns, surrounded by a

96

low stone wall, mark the spot of the execution of Maximilian, Miramon and Mejia. An iron railing formerly topped the wall, but it has been stolen, as well as the inscription tablets. I gathered reverently enough a handful of little stones here and a tuft of brier grass that may have been nourished by the blood of the young Archduke. The ex-convent of Capuchinas, part of which is now used as a, barrack, was his prison. The particular cell he occupied is included in the confines of a private dwelling, walled off from the main building subsequent to those occurrences. The court-martial passed sentence upon him in the Theatre Iturbide, whose stage remains just as it was then. Away across the city, on a sloping rise, stands the old church of La Cruz, which was the Imperial headquarters, and down the lane by its garden wall pointed the one 24—pounder of the besieged, which protected that approach until it was wheeled around by treacherous hands to facilitate the coming of the men of Escobedo, who swarmed into the enclosure through a great breach, whose outlines are still plainly visible in the repaired wall of adobe. The man sent by the lieutenant-colonel to open the doors for us was one who, a lad of 14, had been in the service of the Emperor, and he pointed out in the crumbling wall the nail hole when hung his crucifix, the arrangement of the room and furniture, and the spot where Maximilian stool to be photo be photographed, a day or two before his capture. Two of these old photograph poor of execution and badly fade, were hunted out by Señor de C—and given to me, together with some views made at the time of the siege of some of the points of interest, and also one of the cannonballs improvised "in the days when we had no longer ammunition, and were eating mules and horses." Then I gathered a great bunch of salvia and nicotinium growing between the tiles in the floor of Maximilian's room, unroofed now and open to the weather; and my own camera perpetuated most of the scenes of operation of that time under their present aspect. The whole atmosphere of Queretaro is still redolent of memories of Maximilian. It is a popular belief that the city's commercial decadence is a judgment sent for the shedding of his blood there. They tell, with sobs in the voice, how he died believing that Carlotta died before; of his manly dignity in placing Miramon in the place of honor as they stood ready for execution; and a little while ago the whole city was agitated when, on the death of Father Zoria, his administrators sold the cross of rubies sent him by Maximilian's mother in remembrance of his ministrations to her boy between his doom and his sentence.

Y. H. Addis.

Letter from Yda Addis.

Christmas in Mexico—Posadas.
The Los Angeles Herald. Vol 29, No. 98
8 January 1888.

J had been invited about a month in advance to attend a complete series of *posadas,* including a grand ball, but on the 4th of December I started with some adventurous spirits to make the ascent of Popocatépetl. I made it, too, and was the first of the party to reach the brink of the crater, leaving behind at least one gentleman, stretched on the snow, whimpering like a baby. But the season was a particularly unfavorable one, and the snow was frozen so hard that we were out from 3:30 a. m. until 7:30 p. m, and in consequence both my feet were frozen, one quite badly. It was so swollen that I was unable to wear any footgear except a pair of canoe-shoes of large caliber, which one of the party fortunately had with him. Besides, my face was blistered by the snow-glare, and puffed out till it did not look human. Thus it will be seen that I was in no fit plight for *posadas* and dancing. Stronger reason yet there was a scientific commission going out to explore the famous caverns of Cacahuamilpa, and the thought of not being able to join it inspired me with a profound disgust for all tamer pleasures. The difficulty was lack of transportation, and when twenty-four hours before the start, the chief of the expedition came up to say he could offer mo a scat on top of the diligence, my joy knew no bounds, and I fervently blessed the Minister of Public Works for taking it into his mind to visit the head government astronomer, and thus vacating the seat of that honorable functionary. I had been back from the volcano trip but forty-eight hours, yet, with my face poulticed up for threatened erysipelas, and my "foot in a sling," I perched upon the coach top, and we rolled merrily out of Mexico "while it was yet night." I was the only layman in the party; all the rest wore swells in science. Mr. Frederick Ducane Godman was there, and all the rest were notables, and we had a grand time generally, and that is why I missed the *posadas* this year in Mexico, as on the return I had to take wing for Chihuahua, to spend Christmas with the mother, as per promise. Yet stay! *did* I miss the *posadas* altogether? I had faithfully agreed to stop over from one train to another with friends at Lueritaro, and, walking in without warning, I thought I had mistaken the house. The arches of the corridor were hung with gay banners and lanterns, and even the banana trees in the court and the yellow cat sleeping on the rim of the fountain had an unfamiliarly festal aspect, not congruous with the sedate character of the family. It was not until six girls, all hugging me at once, simultaneously cooed "Oh! how opportune is your arrival! to-night you will break the *piñata*." —Not until then I say, did I realize that they must be holding *posadas*. Being warned that I should have no dinner before 10 p.m., I mildly begged for a cup of chocolate, having brought all my appetite home from the caverns. Shortly after nightfall the guests began to assemble, and a little later they passed into a room set aside for the purpose, and kneeling, prayed and chanted hymns, before the *Nacimiento*. This is a species of shrine, or altar, typifying the great Mystery at Bethlehem, centuries agone. On the summit of an artificial hillock, raised against the wall, in a little chapel, are small images of Joseph and Mary, to which are added on Christmas Eva a figure of the Holy Babe. The little mound is covered with mosses, diversified by little trees, flowers and lakelets formed by bits of looking glass, and it is studded with clay, waxen, or porcelain figures of domestic animals, shepherds, kings and magi, all going up to the worship of the Holy Stranger. Sometimes the arrangement is made a snow scene, by the use of cotton wool, flour, or diamond dust. Concluded the ceremonies before the *Nacimiento*, Joaquinita's guests formed in procession behind two young men, who carried on a platform some of the household wares in the shape of images of favorite patron saints, and, bearing lighted caudles and chanting the Litany, they moved in and out of the different rooms and about the court and corridors, now and then pausing to ask for *posada* [lodging, from which the name of the festival] in memory of the weary search of the Holy Family for shelter at Bethlehem. Finally the march broke up and then social converse and merriment were in order. Fruits, cakes, sweets and other *refrescos* came on the carpet, together with bonhonniecres and trinkets to be carried away as souvenirs. At last arrived the all-important moment for the breaking of the *piñata*, which, be it understood, is cousin-german to the good old-fashioned American grab-bag, dear to the hearts of Sunday school festival people. But the *piñata* is a very apotheosis of grab-bags. Made of clay, or of tissue paper on a bamboo framework, to insure a fragility sufficient to crush under a smart blow, they are modeled after a thousand patterns, and very cleverly are they executed. Cooks, comets, butchers, gigantic roses, brides, turkeys, ballet dancers, fishes, such are some of the varieties I noted among the myriads on sale in the *Zócalo*, or main plaza in Mexico before leaving. It having been decided that I should have the honor of breaking the *piñata*, some maneuvering was necessary to accomplish that end. So the aspirants first blindfolded, wore led wide of the mark, and I am not so sure that the *piñata* was not held aside from them. At last pretty Cholita bandaged my eyes with careful carelessness, and, on the plea of avoiding injury to my lamest foot, held me close up to the doorway, from whose lintel the object of interest was dangling. Even a baseballist could have hit it under such conditions. So the next moment a crowd of youngsters sprawled on the floor, scrambling for the goodies. This concluded the regular ceremonies and the rest of the evening was devoted to music, games and dancing. One contingent remained within doors, while the younger fry adjourned to the ample patio, with its rustling banana-trees, and romped through a series of carpet games not dissimilar to our own. It was nearly midnight when we sat down to a substantial supper, and an hour or more later I lay down, "all booted and saddled," for a brief repose, to rise at 3 a.m.—to board the train bound northward past Chihuahua.

Y. H. Addis.

Letter from Yda Addis

Mexico Industrially, Ecclesiastically, Socially and Benevolently,
Los Angeles Herald, Vol. 30, No. 145
27 August 1888

Editors Herald: —I am often much diverted by the ignorance prevailing among Americans, otherwise clever and well informed, concerning Mexico. Sometimes in the course of relating a mild little anecdote, I have occasion to say, "And so I 'phoned across the town to so-and-so," or "And we took the tramway to such-a-place, twelve miles away, which, of course was much cheaper than a carriage," whereupon the average American who has not visited the country, makes A croquet-arch of his eyebrows, and Bays, "What! Do you have telephones and tramways in Mexico?" And I have even heard said "Of course you must have no such thing as letter-carriers in Mexico," whereas the fact is that one finds telephones in wretched little ranch-towns, twenty leagues from anywhere; every town of any importance along the railways has a tramway plying between the center and the station and about the town, at a fare ranging from 4 to 12 cents, while every point of interest to sightseers near the larger cities are reached by horse cars. As to postal arrangements, the City of Mexico has an ample force of carriers, and the mail is distributed and collected four times daily, or oftener on special occasions. The number of population requisite for the privilege of carrier delivery is smaller than in the United States. Then in the arrangement and fitting up of pupil offices, Mexican towns far surpass American ones of the same size and importance. In providing apparatus and other school supplies, also, the respective officers and committees are very liberal, readily providing the newest and best equipments, and that in abundance. One finds in small class rooms charts, models, etc. Then in the way of benevolent institutions, Mexico is far in advance of the preconceived suppositions of foreigners. Take for instance the charitable establishments at Guadalaxara, a city from which I returned about a fortnight since. There are three establishments there which would compare favorably with corresponding institutions anywhere. The hospital is situated in one of the pleasantest and most salubrious portions of the city, and the building was erected especially for its present use, whereas many such asylums occupy old convent or church buildings whose arrangement is ill-adapted for such purposes. A pleasant portico gives ingress to the building, 185 meters long by 170 wide. It has twenty-three courts,

106

surrounded by noble Tuscan corridors and inclosing pleasant gardens, full of fruits and flowers. Throughout the establishment everything needful for comfort is provided, while nothing is expended on mere luxury—a pleasing contrast to the ostentation too often seen in such places. In the Foundling Home twenty-nine babes were in the hands of the nurses at the time of my visit, and in the Orphan Asylum 134 boys and 186 girls were sheltered, clothed, fed, and taught. They all seemed as healthy and contented as possible, and the smiles and shouts with which they welcomed the matron, Doña Luz Herrera, bespoke the kindness of their treatment, for these little tots are too young to have learned to dissemble. In the School of Arts and Trades for Women are taught the girl inmates of the Hospice of over twelve years of age, as well as outside pupils, who must be girls of good moral conduct between 12 and 18 years old, who may enter with the consent of their parents or guardians. They are taught, beside the common school branches, astronomy, music and foreign languages, lithography, drawing, photography, printing and bookbinding (the printing office conducted by these girls has the contract for the State work in this department); also somewhat of carpentry, the making of *fideos* (a sort of vermicelli-like paste for soups), bread making (the bakery supplies the Hospice and the City Hospital), and the weaving and knitting of hose, ribbons, rebozos (the native head-scarf) and other textiles consumed by the establishment or sold. Then the drawn work, embroidery, etc., made here is most exquisite; so fine it seems as to appear impossible to make by hand. The Home for the Indigent Aged, under the same roof, protects some twenty-eight men and fifty-six women at present; but the noblest department is that which keep 3 girls and women from paths of dishonor by fitting them to earn an independent and honorable living. This Hospice, of which Guadalaxara is so justly proud, and which she so zealously maintains, was founded in 1803 by the then Bishop of that diocese, Juan Cruz Ruiz de Cabanas, whose benevolent face is pictured in the lovely little chapel, whose Ionic dome, at a height of thirty meters, is a topped by a statue of Mercy five meters tall. The city hospital, usually called "Belem" (Bethlehem), was finished in 1792 —the same year of the death of its founder —another Bishop of Guadalaxara, which seems to have been blessed beyond all the rest of Mexico in the matter of churchly magnates. Antonio Alcalde was a Dominican who came from Yucatan in 1786—the year of the great famine in Mexico, owing to frosts which had ruined the crops of the preceding year. During that season this noble Bishop spent $110,000 for corn, which he bestowed upon the poor. His whole life was given up to beneficence. He built schools, more particularly for girls, caused the paving of the city streets, had roads constructed, fostered public instruction, and strove to benefit the people generally, crowning his efforts with the founding of this hospital in the place of the convent of San Miguel de Belem. He used to say that his soul would not be happy in heaven since there would be no poor and wretched there for whom to strive and labor; when he died the entire proceeds of his belongings—clothing, furniture, Episcopal robes and jewels—was $262.25, and his plate consisted of one small silver basin. One feels some faith in the sanctity and sincerity of that sort of churchman! The hospital covers a square of 350 meters. It contains, besides the departments for infectious diseases, six salas or halls, 80x7 meters, radiating like the spokes of a wheel from a central rotunda, an arrangement which insures excellent ventilation and lighting. Three of these halls are known, respectively, as "God, the Father," "God, the Son," and "God, the Holy Ghost," and the walls are liberally decorated with scriptural texts of merciful and tender import—a striking thing where the Roman Catholic religion is still most potent. There are 725 beds, all of iron, and, like all the other appointments, very clean. The average daily movement of patients is ten to twelve; the average number of inmates 275, but at need the establishment can clothe and attend 2,000 patients. The deaths are 20 to 35 monthly. The staff comprises a manager, chaplain, steward, druggist and his assistant, 3 attendant physicians, 70 medical students who reside on the premises for sudden emergencies, and 50 subalterns, nurses etc. There is also the department for the insane, with wards for males, containing 60 patients, and for females, containing 37—all their accommodations being entirely distinct from the rest of the institution. There are also separate infirmaries, as well as schoolrooms, etc., for sick children, and every comfort and convenience in the way of drugstore, baths, etc., etc. On the roof is a meteorological observatory, with all needful instruments.

Rev. John Howland, Congregationalist missionary at Guadalaxara, most kindly placed at the service of our party the excellent horses necessary for his itinerant work, [and I hardly know what we would have done without them, as riding horses, we found, were only to be had for love, not money, in Guada.,] and one wild afternoon, when we had been scampering about for some hours through frequent gusts and squalls and showers, we galloped up to a long, imposing structure at the west side, and found it to be the Penitentiary for which we had been looking. Begun in 1843, by order of Governor Antonio Escobedo, for whom it is named, it is not yet completed, although occupied. It comprises three departments; the offices of the criminal and civil judiciary; the cells, of which there are over 800, and the shops. The edifice is quadrangular, 300x150 meters, with two-storied Doric portico, long lines of heavily barred windows, and turrets for guards at the angles, and it presents a most imposing appearance in its massive, sullen strength. The second or cell department is calculated to contain 3000 comfortably. It is well ventilated, with good hospital, lazaretto, etc. Baths and all other conveniences are provided. An ingenious arrangement is made for the hearing of mass by prisoners in solitary confinement; sixteen galleries, with tiers of cells on either side, radiate from the central chapel, so that the solitaries are not removed from their cells for religious service. In the shops are carried on the trades of carpentry, shoemaking, tinnery, cooperage, brass working, hats and other straw work, and weaving, eighteen looms being occupied with the manufacture of *rebozos*, *zarapes*, (head-scarves and blankets) besides the cotton cloth used for the trousers, blouse and beret, which, with good shoes, constitutes the prison uniform. The women work in a separate department, besides preparing the food of the institution. In schools taught by the most modern systems, the prisoners are taught such branches, in conjunction with the trades in which they are Instructed, will fit them for becoming good citizens at the expiration of terms, and to the same end, and to promote industry, each prisoner receives with his liberty twenty-five per cent of his earnings while in prison. The inmates are provided with good, wholesome food, and all practicable comforts and they appear as contented as men deprived of heir liberty may be. A guard, civil and of state troops, of some fifty strong, watches over the prison. I think that the magnitude and system of these initiations, described necessarily with great imperfection in a paper of this descriptions, will perhaps dispel some erroneous ideas, and that good Angeleños will agree with me that such achievements are fairly good for "benighted Mexico."

Y. H. Addis. August, 1888.

Mexican Lustred Pottery

By
Y. H. Addis
Photo by Y. H. Addis
Appeared *Harper's* Vol. LXXIX
June-Nov 1889

My attention was called by an American visitor in Mexico, some two years ago, to remarkable specimens of iridescent pottery which he had found at Patzcuaro. It was known that it was manufactured somewhere in Mexico by Indian potters, but he could obtain no clew to the place of the factory. I undertook at the time to make inquiries both as to the place and the process of this manufacture.

After a year of investigation I found that San Felipe was the source of *loza irisada*—and an occasional detail tended to distinguish among numerous towns and villages of that name one with the surname *Torresmochas* (Incomplete Towers) in the state of Guanaxuato. I had found the supply of the ware small, and this scarcity, together with the fact that each variety of Mexican pottery is peculiar to a certain district, to which it is readily referable, led, with other collateral evidence, to the conclusion that this sort emanated from one place only.

In the capital city of Guanaxuato the information obtainable concerning the objective point was still vague and meager. The impression given was that San Felipe of the Unfinished Towers was a small and remote mining camp. I was also warned that the Indians, who are the potters, are shy, surly, secretive, and very suspicious of strangers. So it was with no little misgiving that I set out for San Felipe, under escort of a party going thither on business.

The distance from Guanaxuato is only some sixty-five miles, yet we were in the saddle six days, during four of which we made only the inevitable stops; this because of the broken character of the country, and the bad roads, which constrain the traveler to slow riding. The way lay in great part through a wild mountainous region, said to be infested with bandits; we feared them not, nor saw any. The people we met were simple, respectful peasants, sincere, hospitable, and kindly— typical mountaineer people. The trail was rough, in some places dangerous; but all of our little band were seasoned travelers, and we found the novelty pleasing and the hardships piquant.

On nearing San Felipe great was our surprise to find it a thriving town of some 11,000 or 12,000 inhabitants, a picturesque little city lying in a wide, fruitful valley, and plying a distinct and considerable commerce with the outlying districts. Here pottery-making, instead of being the vital industry, is only a detail, albeit one of sufficient importance.

Here again, at the fountain-head, the subject was lighted most faintly. The ware was abundant enough, but it was not a favorite variety with housewives, probably owing to its brittleness, and its aesthetic value was not taken into account.

The views of our entertainers—Don Narciso E., the leading merchant and banker, with his circle of acquaintance—concurred with those of certain European *savants* long residents of Guanaxuato, viz., that the Indian makers, being of suspicious and jealous nature, would refuse to afford us any enlightenment. These friends kindly chaperoned us to the factory—that is to say, to the adobe corral where the work was in progress—and once the place was reached, sat down with an "I wash my hands of the business and wish you well out of it" air that was not inspiring of hopefulness.

Among the many potteries of San Felipe we found but one making the iridescent ware. The kiln was a structure of adobe, or sun-dried brick, some six feet high, on a base of perhaps eight feet square. The manufacture was carried on in the open air, or in the brush huts that shouldered a few fruit trees in the enclosure, and the paraphernalia was the raw material, the simplest of lathes, and a long pole with a hook on the end for lifting the ware while hot after firing. The chief potter was a lithe but sturdy fellow, apparently of almost pure Indian blood, who spoke Spanish but indifferently. He had on a pair of ancient overalls, a tattered "merino knitted under-vest," a battered greasy hat set well over the bridge of his nose, and rawhide sandals. Around his neck and over his bare brown breast depended a rosary made from the gray berried of a plant known in old-fashioned gardens, called "Job's-tears." He was assisted by diverse women and urchins shy as antelopes. We installed ourselves on the ground with infinite composure, and our time being limited, at once set up the camera that had traveled out from Guanaxuato upon the brawny shoulders of Pancho, the porter, whom we paid the extravagant sum of three reals (thirty-seven and a half cents) per day "and find himself" for carrying this and some hundred pounds of other matters. It is certain that these Indians had never seen or heard of a photographic outfit, but they complied with a fair grace with the stereotyped request to "keep perfectly still, and do not move the least little bit until I tell you."

The negatives secured, I proceeded to question them; and as we talked, little by little the air of startled distrust wore away, and, to the extreme surprise of the visitors, Mexicans as well as American, the workers became positively communicative, not to say enthusiastic. They told me freely the ingredients of their preparations, bringing me samples of each component part, "because you might not know what we mean by our name for it," rating the cost and the profits per gross on each class of vessel, and urging me to await the unloading of the kiln, then in firing. The process, then, of making the ware is as follows: the vessels, once molded, are fired, and when thoroughly cold are glazed with a mixture of (1) oxide of lead; (2) broken glass, which they buy from refuse shops; (3) "peacock copper"; and (4) a very fine sand found near San Felipe. It was impossible to obtain even an approximately accurate idea of the proportions employed, because the potters have so long worked by the rule of thumb that they are really incapable of describing the quantities. Therefore this point would have to be determined by examination during their practical working. After application of the glaze comes a second firing—the one in progress at the time of the visit. The ware emerged from the kiln at this stage dull and clouded, of a thick muddy brown or greenish color. As rapidly as possible they buried the pieces in a great heap of stable manure, and after from one to two hours' repose in this substance they were disinterred, transformed by the ammoniacal fumes to the lustrous brilliance, with the shifting, varying hues that glean on the breast of the peacock. The secret, if secret there be, seems to lie in two of the elements of the glaze, in combination with the ammonia treatment, for I am skeptical as to the potter's assertion that the effect is due

distinguishing trait seems to be that, at least when baked, of brittleness, as I have found in my cost by experiments in shipping and by observation at the pottery, where the ground was almost completely covered by the *débris* of freshly broken vases, cups, plaques, candlesticks, and censers. Illustrates the character of these people; I received many felicitations on the success of my exploit, when happy issue was attributed by the courtier-like Mexicans to the power of personal influence and "sympathetic charm." This was flattering, but to me not conclusive or satisfactory, and an after-occurrence furnished me with an explanation which is plausible and I think the true one. Having to choose between extra raiment and the camera in the matter of luggage, I elected to take the camera, and so had to adapt my riding-habit to the requirements of walking.

118

The long simple folds and severe finish caused these unsophisticated creatures to mistake me for a nun, and they could, I take it, refuse nothing to one of the venerated "little mothers, whom they have seen so seldom since the establishment of the reform laws abolished convents in Mexico. I felt myself rank imposter and unspeakably guilt when I discovered the deception I had a innocently practiced to achieve my little triumph in winning a secret that has been handed down in this out-of-the-way corner, no doubt, since it was taught there to the Indians by some artist-souled priest of the conquistadores.

Killed by Apaches

News Received of the Death of Seven Persons.

A private letter was received from Chihuahua yesterday by Miss Yda Addis, containing advices of a terrible tragedy that had been perpetrated in that State.

Appeared in *Los Angeles Herald* Volume 33, Number 95, January 15, 1890.

About five days ago a party of hunters came upon the bodies of seven men, near Ptacnik's mines, in the north-western section of Chihuahua, just beyond the Tarahumara country. From the fact that each of the bodies was pierced by arrows, some of which still remained in the wounds, and also that the heads of the victims had been badly crushed, the massacre from undoubtedly by the bloody Apache Indians, whose custom is to complete their deadly work in this manner. When the news reached Chihuahua, inquiries were made as to the identity of the party whose members had met such an untimely death, and as Ptacnik and his son, with five miners, had left for the mines some weeks before, it was concluded that theirs must have been the ill-fated party whose corpses had been discovered on the plains. This supposition was verified to a certain extent by the fact that telegrams which had been dispatched to the station, at which they were due, had not been answered.

Edward Ptacnik, the owner of the mines which bear his name, was by birth a Pole, but ban resided in the United States and Mexico for about thirty years past, during which time he has amassed a considerable fortune as a merchant, exclusive of that derived from his mines, which are considered as the richest in the northern part of the State of Chihuahua. He was a highly educated gentleman, with strong literary and scientific tastes, and should he have met the fate which he so little deserved, his loss will be an almost irreparable one to the community in which he lived. His wife, a remarkably clever lady, and family of nine children, are anxiously awaiting a confirmation of their worst fears, as but little hope is entertained of the escape of their relatives.

Alfred Shea Addis's Dispatches from Arizona and New Mexico Territories....

South-Eastern Arizona

What an *Old Californian* Says About the
Mines of Tombstone District
Appeared in *The Inter Ocean* (Chicago, Illinois) 5 June 1879,
Page 8,

The interest in the mines of the Tombstone District is growing wonderfully along the far Southwestern and Western border. An intelligent and observant traveler, Mr. A. S. Addis, writes some excellent letters, which the Arizona *Star* of Tucson, prints, and which will be found of value to those who have been looking toward Southern Arizona as the new mining country, which is looming up in the Western horizon.

He gives some interesting facts about the far Southwest, and says of Tucson that it is one of the best-governed towns on the frontier—no rowdyism, no drunkenness on the streets, no man for breakfast, no revolvers in sight. The climate is described as delightful, pleasantly warm days, and cool nights. The doctors are said to be growing fat, wearing out their clothes waiting, waiting for patients, and the lawyers get rich on great fees for mining papers. This same gentleman speaks of the Tombstone Mining

District, which, as is well known, is some seventy-five miles from Tucson. The principal mines, he says, at the Contention, the Lucky Cuss, the Laugh Nut, and about a dozen others of acknowledged richness. It is stated that there is a ten-stamp mill running, it having commenced work about a week before Mr. Addis wrote his letter. On third-class ore it averaged $100 per ton assay. He states that one mine along has on the dump 1,200 tons of rock, which assays $150 per ton. The whole face of the earth is one immense deposit. Several shafts have been sunk from thirty to 150 feet showing well-defined walls, the veins growing larger and richer as they descend, proving them to be true fissure veins. "Nothing," he says, "seen in my travels in Mexico, Nevada or California equals it, not excepting the famous Comstock lodes. Were they in Nevada, they would command millions, and there would be a town of 5,000 or 6,000 people, but that is simply a matter of time. What has appeared a drawback in the past has been met, and arrangements have just been completed at the East, by several enterprising parties, by which the entire Tombstone District will be supplied with an abundance of the best water. It is announced that another fifteen-stamp mill will soon be ready for work, and the camp will be a brisk one before long.

←——————→

June 9, 1879, Evening Express

SOUTHERN ARIZONA

[Special Correspondence Express]

TUCSON THE GREAT CENTER.

In ancient times all roads led to Rome; in this, all towns pay tribute to Tucson, the business center of Southern Arizona, which justly boasts of being the best governed town of any frontier; no rowdyism or drunkenness on the streets, no man for breakfast, no revolvers in sight. Her Mayor, Mr. Toole, one of her wealthiest citizens, got tired of the monotonous sameness, and wanted to resign, but, by unanimous request of Council and citizens, was hindered in so doing. So he has to serve an indefinite term. If any one commits a crime, he is yanked up and sent to Yuma to cool off.

The streets are kept clean, and water carts run all day. Where can you find its equal? The climate is simply delightful, getting about as hot as you can have it in the City of the

Angels, but from eve to morning cool and pleasant, needing a blanket during the night—the air dry and pure—just the thing for poor consumptives. The Doctors grow fat, wearing out their pants waiting for patients. Lawyers grow fat and saucy on big fees for mining papers and divorce suits, some of which have created great scandal here and at Frisco; for these your readers can read the *Chronicle,* for particulars, as I wish to deal in the mining talk, upon which you can place reliance, as I am not paid to lie or "set-down aught in malice."

Tombstone District, which is now the exciting subject, is some 75 miles north of here. The principal mines are the Tombstone, Lucy Cuss, Tough Nut and about a dozen more of acknowledged richness; the first three are owned by the following parties: Safford, Gird, Bonburg, Schieffelin and Bros., and the Corbin Bros., of St. Louis and the East, who have put up a stamp mill, which commenced running about five days ago on third-class ore, averaging $100 per ton assay. The mill gets out about 80 per cent, fineness 960; this is one of the richest districts in the territory. If I should tell you my opinion, you would scarcely think it credible, but I will state that one mine alone has on the dump twelve hundred tons of rock which assays over $150 per ton. The whole face of the earth is one immense deposit. Several shafts have been sunk from thirty to one hundred and fifty feet, showing well defined walls, the veins growing larger and richer as they descend, proving them to be true fissure veins. Nothing seen in my travels in Mexico, Nevada, or California equals it, not excepting the famous Comstock lodes. Were they in Nevada they would command millions, and there would be a town of 5,000 or 6,000 people, but 'tis simply a matter of time. The mill is A No. 1; the running is a success and will be sending out bricks by the dozen. The California capitalists will rue the day when they gave the Eastern capitalists the first deal, as there are no shares for sale. The only drawback is the scarcity of water for working all the mines, but there is double the amount for the one mill completed. Another mill of fifteen stamps will soon be ready for work, when large dividends will be declared, as the members of the company give it their personal attendance, and don't rust to manipulating Superintendents.

Patagonia District embraces the Harshaw, Holland, and many other rich lodes that assay from $30 up to $250; this is also about seventy miles distant.

Papago District is away some sixty five miles. The Desert claim is gold-bearing, showing quite freely in the rock. Pacheco mine is silver, being black sulphurets, showing very rich.

Oro Blanco District, at about an equal distance as the above, embraces the Flood and Kirkpatrick group, Empire and Yellow Jacket lodes, and many others, all showing good lodes and giving good assays. Baboquivari Nos. 1, 2 and 3. The lode runs under an immense porphyry dyke. This is silver-bearing, assaying from $25 to $1,500. In the same district are the Nicholson lode, Silver Peak and many others all showing true fissures and mineral of untold wealth.

In the near distance we have the Poor Man's lode, in the Tucson range of mountains, showing an average vein of twelve feet, assaying from $25 to $850.

These are simply a few of the most noted mines that have been developed; besides many others, too numerous to mention. Miners are daily making new discoveries in different direction near here. The country is not yet prospected, but I would advise no miner to come unless he has the currency to pay his expenses, as it takes money to live here; and as capital is slow of investment and mills are few, he might starve while being a bloated millionaire. but if he has the energy and stamps to stand the siege, and don't love mescal or other similar concomitants on which many a miner here has clogged his stamps, then come along.

For mechanics it is no place. The principal buildings are adobe, which the natives excel in building. I counted yesterday some forty-two new buildings under construction. A small room 10 x 12 brings $15 per month, and scarce at that.

Mining suit—Yesterday a suit was decided before Judge French, about the Sidney mine, of the Tombstone group, located over two years ago by Mitchell & Co., who failed to record in the sixty-days; relocated by Gifford & Ames; original locaters brought suit for ejectment; granted by the Court on the ground that it was not necessary to record if the monuments had been put up and the work required done on the claim. This is a good precedent, as it will stop that curse of all mining camps—jumping.

A. S. A.

L. to R: John Philip Clum (1st Mayor of Tombstone, founder of the *Tombstone Epitaph*) and Wyatt Earp.
Photo from *True West Archives*

Indians scouts with the American Military

Photo by A. S. Addis, from the collection of the
photo historian Carl Chafin

January 26, 1880, Evening Express,

SILVER CITY

Her Mines—Tributary—Camps Business Prospects—Indian Raids—San Carlos Agency—Rascally Commissioners—Thieving Agents—Honest Man not Wanted—Express and Stage Extortions—Good Advice to Southern Pacific Railroad—Jewish Marriage in High Life—A Rachael of Morality.

[Correspondence Express]

SILVER CITY, This well-named camp lies in a beautiful basin surrounded on all sides by rolling hills, until in a distance of eight miles rises the lofty peaks of the Pinos Altos range. All these hills and mountains are packed with ore of a high grade; in fact, the city itself rests in peace over untold millions.

You can hardly pick up a rock anywhere and break it without finding minerals in it. In the "Legal Tender"—one of the first mines located—the exterior lines of which adjoin those of the patented town site, the ore consists of carbonates and sulphates, assaying from $150 to $860. Some

133

selected specimens sent to New York went as high as $12,040. This is one of the mines now owned by the Massachusetts and New Mexico Mining Company. They have many others that will prove equally as good.

THE CHLORIDE DISTRICT

Is situated about two and a half miles from the town, and its mines are principally owned by M. W. Bremen, who may safely be called the father of the town and camp, as he stuck to it through all the difficulties and can safely now claim his millions. He is blamed by some for not heralding his good lick and inviting others to come, but his course was legitimate as he wanted to purchase all he could himself. It would take too much space to particularize the good mines here, as they are many, five hundred locations having been made this last month. No more favorable place can be found for capitalists to invest, as water is plenty, wood costing only $2.50 per cord, and an endless supply almost at their doors. Mining here now costs only $6 per ton. With the latest improved machinery, this could be reduced one-third. Strange as it may appear, while Arizona is overrun with idle miners, none can be had here, while wages are equally good and living much cheaper. But as I have diverged from the town, I will now try and describe it:

SILVER CITY

Is a well laid off town, covering an area of 320 acres.

The streets run east, west, north and south. The houses are principally brick and adobe, with shingles roofs. There are many tasty dwellings and not a vacant house or room in the town. Many newcomers camp out, as the weather is as lovely as May. There are two good hotels having from thirty to forty rooms, well furnished and well kept. Board and lodging is $10 a week, just $4 cheaper than Tucson. There are three good restaurants. Two good mills are running and another will be in operation in February. A large planning mill is running night and day. There is also a foundry and machine shops, three groceries, two drug stores and enough whisky shops, a dance hall, two unfinished churches; no preaching; plenty of lawyers and doctors, no dentist. While it may appear a strange contradiction of morality, having no preacher, yet all stores are compelled to close on Sunday, and for quietness on Sunday I will defy any old Puritan town to excel Silver City. If a saloon keeps open its proprietor is fined. Whether the Court pays the fine back deponent *sayeth* not.

THE CLIMATE

Cannot be excelled anywhere. Silver City has had but two deaths in six weeks. These cases were of men who bucked against whiskey, and, as usual, got the worst of it. The doctors and druggist complain of it being fearfully healthy, and were it not cases of fever coming from the Gila and other areas the aforesaid gentlemen would have poor picking. As you have been informed by telegraph.

THE RED DEVILS

Are again at their favorite work of killing and robbing. Major Morrow, with the colored troops, is after them, but as the noble reds don't fear the Buffalo soldiers, as they call them, nobody will get "muchly" hurt. The universal opinion of those who live on the frontier is that colored troops are unfit for Indian service. Major Morrow, who is known by those who have been with him in action, to be a brave officer, has no chance whatever with the wily foe. For instance, a short time since, knowing himself to be near the foe, he gave the order to advance, and led off himself, when upon coming within sight of the reds, he turned to order an advance, and found that all his troops had found cover—he alone being exposed to fire; I imagine he felt as I did while traveling in Mexico. Some ninety persons thirsty being eighty miles in a desert, no water, no shelter to serve as refuge—nothing good worked out of it.

The raids result from Indian agents' dishonesty and the difficulty appointing an honest man. This may seem harsh language, but 'tis true, as can be proven by late exposures in Arizona. Even Commissioner Hoyl had laws passed to gosbie a mine on the reservation of San Carlos. They had one honest agent there—J. P. Clum—who took the agency when in its worst plight, who fearlessly went to work and brought order

136

out of chaos, compelled the Indians to behave themselves, organized Indians to fight Indians, fought and killed many of the bad ones, gave them what they were entitled to in annuities, and had peace for many months; but he was harassed by jealousy on the part of those who wanted his place until he resigned. Another was appointed to his place who in a few months, was court-martialed for dishonest. Immediately after the ejection of Clum...

VICTORIO AND HIS BAND

Left the reservation and have been raiding ever since. Within a radius of 100 miles of this place has killed 111 persons, fearfully mutilating women and children after outraging them. And sill old granny Schurz wants to make peace with them. Out of such a dastardly Government that won't protect her people! Had such outrages been perpetrated on English subjects a whole nation of barbarians would have been annihilated. Even poor misruled Mexico, does better, offering $100 for every scalp of these demons. It costs Uncle Sam about one million dollars and two hundred lives for every Indian Killed. This is no exaggeration.

EXPRESS AND STAGE COMPANIES,

As I promised a few lines to these cormorants, and as I don't think the railroads abound get all the blame going, I will say a word or two relative to what is known as Wells, Fargo & Co.s Express, which is a misnomer. It should be called 'Sharon

& Flood' Express, as Sharon and Flood own nearly all the stock in the original company. Sharon has the cheek to get money under false pretense of being Nevada's Senator. These express agents have the cheek to charge twenty cents per pound for freight from San Francisco to Tucson, except when Uncle Sam comes into competition in four pounds lots and carries it for sixteen cents. To beat Uncle Sam they will carry small packages, such as could go by mail, at the same rates. The stage company that runs to this point charges 8 cents per pound for every 100 miles, 450 miles to Santa Fé, cost 36 cents; to Chicago, 12 cents; total, 48 cents per pound. From San Francisco to Tucson, 29 cents; thence here, 16 9-10 cents. Now, Uncle Sam, being more liberal, carries all mailable freight for 16 cents per pound, thus compelling these generous carriers to run empty; whereas, if they would charge a reasonable price they would get all. Why don't the Southern Pacific Railroad Company adopt the express business as the Union Pacific done? The Union Pacific cleared last year from this business $270,000—a nice plum to divide among her stockholders.

OUTLYING TOWNS.

I intended to tell something about the towns tributary to this place, but will simply name them and their distance and will write you fully when I visit them. First is Pinos Altos— 8 miles distance north; 200 in habitants; placer and gold quartz, yielding about $2,000 per week. Georgetown—20 miles west; 400 inhabitants. Silver Camp, 2 small mills yielding from $4,000 to $6,000 per week. There is some high grade ore here, going as high as $20,000 per ton. Full description hereafter. Clifton—100 miles northwest—the great copper camp. Three million dollars worth of copper has been shipped from this camp, all passing through Silver City.

HYMEN.

In conclusion of this article: Lastly, and thirteenthly, I will say we have a wedding to-day in Jewish high life. A Morganatic daughter of one of the copper kings is the bride, and thereby hangs a pleasant tale. The father of the bride, years ago, when he first came here was poor, and, women being scarce, took, as was usual in those days, one of the fairest of the dusky race of Aztecs to live with him. After many years, and when comparatively rich, he went to Europe, married a fair Jewess, and brought her here. This wife, finding her husband had a daughter by his former companion, sought her out, took her home, educated and treated her as her own child. The consequence is that to-day she is married to one of the leading Jewish merchants. Surely this Mother in Israel is a Rachael at the well of morality deserving a crown of white roses worked in gold. What an example to some of her people who live in Tucson, and who treat the children of their husbands by former companions or wives with contempt and loathing.

As you may find this article too long, take it in sections as I had to do with a six-footer wanting his picture full length.

Yours, etc.   A. S. A.

United States Senator from Nevada William Sharon,
By Mathew Brady - Library of Congress Prints and Photographs Division. Brady-Handy Photograph Collection.

May 6, 1880, Evening Express

CLIFTON, ARIZONA.

On the Trail—Africans and Aborigines—Victorio's Trail—Burro Springs—Indian Murders—A Would-be Here—The Gila River—Wandering Joe—A Strange Being, Who is He?—Where the Hurricanes are Made—Copper is King —Twisted Lightening.

[Correspondence Express.]

DEAR EXPRESS: Although long silent, I have not forgotten you. I daily receive your kindly reminder. Since my last I have visited Fort Bayard, and been initiated into all the mysteries of bloody war (?). Returning to Silver City after a stay of two weeks, I took up the back trail to Tucson, starting from Silver City on April 8th. On the second day my team gave out five miles from...

BURRO SPRINGS,

The chosen haunt of Victorio's murdering band. My assistant went for relief to the Burro station, while I took my needle gun and got behind a rock, to wait for three hours for him to return. As I was in sight of the Indian trail, you can rest assured there was not much romance in the situation. After help came we started again, got within a mile and a half of the Springs, when (thanks to one of the Silver City's botch blacksmiths) down went a wheel. Had to go after another wagon to carry the traps to the stations. In this last distance we passed many crosses, the evidence of several bloody massacres, by the Indians. The last was a Mexican Circus troupe of eight persons, returning to Silver City from Clifton. They were all ambushed and murdered, even the poor trick dogs of the company. Right here I will give you something promised in a former article.

GEN. HATCH AND HIS MEN AGREIE.

This would be hero who withheld the sickening confessions of Mr. and Mrs. Meeker, for fear the frontiersmen would hang the murderous red devils, as they passed through Colorado to Washington to be petted by Granny Schurz, has been trying to gain paper notoriety as a brilliant Indian fighter. As he has proved in every instance a perfect failure. I believe in giving him the benefit he desires in a left handed way. 'Tis true his mounted dragoons have proved a perfect success in eating up Uncle Sam's grub and killing all the horses, hiding from Victorio's cutthroats, and drinking up Satire's bad whiskey. Since my visit to Fort Bayard, I am more fully convinced of the inefficiency of the colored troops and the

142

officers who pretend to command them. I couldn't think of a

... A GREATER FARCE,

Could be perpetrated by any government than our participation invading the Indians. They captured the stores and howitzer. After keeping the gun several days and finding that they could not use it, they smeared it with excrement and left it for the menagerie to recapture. The brilliant plan this...

MIGHTY INDIAN CATCHER

Is now to place fifty men at every spring, send Indian allies to drive poor Vic. from his mountain fastness, and corral him. While he is carrying out this grand campaign Vic. slips down and murders a few more settlers. All the force this noble General wants to assist him is three thousand troops and three hundred Indian allies—all to whip Vic's band of less than 150 Indian thieves. While all this glitter of war is going on the Government is feeding Victoria's squaws and young snakes at the San Carlos Agency. Surely we have a

FINE BENEVOLENT GOVERNMENT

Had we a Gen. Harney or Col. Chivington how seen would this question be settled, and the poor settler and miner could live in peace. Must the pioneer forever suffer on account of a lot of thieving imbeciles at Washington City? There will be a terrible reckoning before long if this matter is not stopped. After staying at Burro Springs for four days waiting for repairs we again started and got to the...

GILA RIVER.

To fully describe this tortuous stream is beyond my power. Imagine a swift running river about 60 feet wide. Somebody is crossing it about fifteen minutes, going down a jump-off about four feet and coming up on the other five or six feet. You can depend upon it that some of the tallest cussing is done here of any point in the world. Teams sometimes take days to cross. The fantastic gestures of drivers, their loud *carajos* and cracking of whips, yelling and screeching, you would imagine the devil had broken loose. Thinking that amongst them I recognized an old acquaintance, I crossed a fallen tree, went up to get a good look, and sure enough it proved to be ...

WANDERING JOE.

A strange, mysterious white man, whom I first met in Kansas during the bloody times, afterwards in Montana, ten years ago in Mexico, and here, again. He had told me part of his life, which I had to promise not to divulge without his consent. This I can say—that this strange being is never known to sleep in-doors; carries to blankets; has long, unkempt hair and whiskers; always pays for what he gets; has money and never works. I asked him where he was going, and he said to hunt diamonds. He carries a bundle of papers which he has promised to give me sometime. As I have met him in so many odd places, I sometimes think he must be my

144

spook. If he is, he is a well-disposed one, as he always brings me good luck. Should I be so fortunate as to get his permit, I will give you his life's history. He is surely a strange being.

Leaving the Gila to the right, we took the road over the mountains. Some of them that we crossed recalled Christian's trip, described in Bunyan's Pilgrim's progress. After ascending and descending many lofty summits, we at last came to a rugged peak at least 5,000 feet high, and with a fearful descent of about 45 degrees, we came to the San Francisco river, which we followed about three miles, till we arrived at...

CLIFTON.

The scenery on this river will equal the Apennines for grandeur and ruggedness. Here are such boldly depicted ruined castles and ancient fortresses as you will find in no other spot in North America. Here a (Albert) Bierstadt could spend months in glorious studies nowhere equaled. Clifton is the copper king of Americas. Here everything in the way of development is carried on in the most primitive manner imaginable. A furnace not much larger than a good-sized coffee mill gives employment and life to at least one thousand persons. The only thing that looks modern is a narrow-gauge railroad, six miles in length, reaching from the furnace to the mines, and this is run by mule power.

THE LONGFELLOW MINING CO.,

Consisting of Henry and Charles Lisinsky, and J.

Trudenthall, of New York, are turning out a clear profit of $2,000 per day. They employ about 400 persons in the mines, paying from $1.75 to $2.50 to Mexicans and Chinamen; the latter in Mexican dollars, which the company buys at 15 percent discount. The Mexicans get half orders on store and half Mexican dollars for what is due them. As there is not much due them each week—as they are proverbial for running in debt—as they don't get much cash. As a sample of prices I will give you a few: Molasses, $3 per gallon; flour $8 per 100 lbs.; a decoction called whiskey, $4 per bottle.

TWISTED LIGHTENING.

Could I get a recipe for this decoction called whisky said here I would attach a wire to the North Pole and outrival Edison in furnishing light to this benighted world. The furnace above mentioned on any Sunday and Monday night after pay day would give a glorious Representation of Dante's Hell—its lurid green light, shinning upon the waters, making them look like molten lava. The wild gestures of the feeders, their demonic yells and contortions, cannot be equaled on earth.

GOLD CAMP,

As there is a great excitement about the above camp and placer diggings—five miles north—I will defer a description till my next article. A

Hoping you are not wearied by my stories, I am yours,

A. S. A

146

Colonel John Milton Chivington

January 27, 1821, Lebanon, Ohio
October 4, 1894, Denver, Colorado

Henry Lisinsky,
Born in Poland 1836;
Died in New York 1924.

June 7 1880, Evening Express

[Correspondence Express]

INDIAN BUCHERIES IN NEW MEXICO

Backward Movement—Death on the Trail—Consternation on Every Hand—
Have we a Government.

EDITOR EXPRESS:—In my letter from Clifton I promised you a more definite description of the mines in eastern Arizona. After visiting Gold Camp, about six miles west of Clifton, I started for the Gila River country, striking it at a point known as Pueblo Viejo. The road from Clifton to this place is considered one of the most dangerous on account of the many Indian murders that have been committed. After leaving the river, we passed through a cañon where is located Ash Springs, a favorite haunt of these murdering devils. The cañon is marked on both sides by piles of stones, mounted with crosses, showing where the many murders have been done. When I arrived at Solomanville I learned of a fresh murder a few days before my arrival. The Deputy Sheriff of Apache County, Arizona, who was out on a collecting tour with a companion, was murdered and horribly mutilated. A few days after my arrival the news came of another terrible massacre on the Frisco River, some twenty miles distant, in which...

A WHOLE SETTLEMENT WERE BUTCHERED.

Over fifteen persons are known to have been killed. Hearing of death and Indians on every hand, I concluded to try and get back to Silver city, some 100 miles distant. Starting in company with two men named Hildebrand and Carson, who were going after goods to Las Cruces. By extreme cautiousness we traveled safely till we came to the forks of roads where one branched to Silver City, some 18 miles distant, the other to Las Cruces. The day after I left the party they were attacked and both killed and burned, besides some five others whom they had caught up with—all were killed and burned with the wagons and their contents.

CONSTERNATION REIGNS

On every hand, Settlers and miners are gathering together for safety. No one is safe in Eastern Arizona or Western New Mexico. All mining interest and farming is paralyzed. In the name of God and justice, when will this reign of terror and death end! Must all the poor settlers and miners be butchered, while a lot of thieving office-seekers are laying plans for more swindling of the people? Have we a Government? *I say no,* not while this old imbecile Hatch, who is not fit to command a band of geese, is strutting around like an old turkey-gobbler, sending false dispatches and refusing ammunition to parties who would fight these devils incarnate. Murder is being done on every hand.

CAPT. PARKER,

With his Indian scouts, came upon this band of murderers a few days before the massacre at Fort Cummings, surrounded them and killed many. Running out of ammunition he sent to Hatch for more, but he would not send it. He, however, rushed off to the nearest red tape telegraph office and telegraphed a victory over the Indians by his Ninth menagerie, when he was not within forty miles of them. Now, these are simply facts, and I don't want them withheld, as the military telegraph will allow nothing to pass the lines of derogatory to them.

As I do not feel like describing more, while death lurks on every hand, I will defer handling that subject till some other time.

Yours, in haste,

A. S. A.

Silver City, June 1, 1880.

Catherine Antrim's home in Silver City, New Mexico; she
was Billy the Kid's mother.
Photograph by Alfred Shea Addis

June 12, 1880, Evening Express

Silver City

Clifton—Gold Camp—Gila River—Some More Indians—
A Dawn of Hope
—Silver City—Her Advance—Her Wants—
A Good Country for Miners and Mechanics

[Correspondence of the Express]

EDITOR EXPRESS: Having promised your readers a more full description of Clifton and Gold Camp, I shall attempt to fill the bill. Clifton, the center of the great copper mines of Arizona, was, some four years ago, but little known in mining circles. It was discovered by a Mr. Metcalf and some partners. Afterwards the discoverers took into partnership the Lesinsky brothers, Henry and Charles, and F. Prudenthale, of Las Cruses. After considerable prospecting had been done some dissatisfaction arose between the original discoverers and the moneyed parties, the result of which was that the moneyed parties got the mines, with Henry Lesinsky as manager.

ON THE DOWN GRADE.

Notwithstanding his being a good business man the Company got into debt about one hundred and seventy thousand dollars, owing to the decline in the price of copper. Lesinsky, having the capacity equal to a Wall Street broker, established a store, paying the Mexican employees in orders for goods. You can assume that the goods were disposed of at good profits. While the pay seemed good, the actual expense was not over 60 cents per day to each hand. Then copper took an upward hand. Then copper took an upward tendency from 11 to 15 cents per pound; then again 22 and 25 cents per pound; and in an almost incredible space of time the Company was out of debt and making money. As copper maintains its price, and the shrewd financial management is little modified, they are coining money. Charles Lesinsky, the present manager, is more liberal than his brother, the miners reaping the benefit of the change.

AN INSPECTION OF THE MINES.

I took the cars that run from the Furnace, situated on the San Francisco river, some seven miles from the mines, and after ascending 600 feet came to the mine. Here truly is a busy scene. Pack burros with water that has to be transferred up the hill to the mines; Chinamen with barrows of ore going from the mine to the dump; Mexican assorters of ore; bosses frantically gesturing and trying to make the men *sabe*—all form a truly diverting scene. Entering the mine, which is finely arched at the entrance, with its many tunnels in different directions, you can in their various deviations wander for over four miles beneath the surface, many of the shafts sinking hundreds of feet. The ore is principally found in pockets, as there is no defined ledge. a great deal of prospecting has to be done to find these pockets, but when found they pay immensely. Had I the naming of the mine I would have called it the Grand Prospect instead of the Longfellow, but I presume they will find it long enough before they get to the bottom. After enjoying some fine views I returned to Clifton for a visit to...

GOLD CAMP.

This camp is about six miles from Clifton, southeast. Many rich discoveries of gold quartz and placers have been found, but on account of Indians this camp is almost deserted. Amongst the refugees is John Eberle, formerly of Los Angeles, who I understand lost his camp outfit. Clifton Camp is at least 100 miles from Silver City, and not adjoining as erroneously stated, It will undoubtedly be a good camp—when Hatch allows the Indians to quit killing white men.

THE GILA RIVER COUNTRY.

Arriving at Solomonville, about the center of one of the largest bends of the Gila, I found a magnificent farming valley, ranging from one to three miles in width, probably some 14 miles long, a large, broad water ditch running the whole length. Here last year was raised and sold over four million pounds of grain, besides potatoes, corn, etc. The section strongly reminds me of the Gospel Swamp country.

SOLOMONVILLE

Is named after I. E. Solomon, who came here about four years ago with a capital of about four hundred dollars in goods, furnished by the Lesinskys. He is now worth at least seventy thousand dollars. His profits from furnishing coal to the Longfellow Company are at least two hundred dollars per month. As he is an energetic hard-worker, he deserves it all. His hospitable doors are always open to the deserving. May he the sad fate of his poor employees, who were killed at the Fort Cummings massacre.

SILVER CITY.

On my return here, I found a perfect hive of industry. In my absence, some fourteen houses had been built, and some twenty-eight more were under contract. Not a room was to be had at any price. Had it not been for this Indian massacre we would have doubled our population this year.

Many new branches of business have been started, among which another newspaper, that, in a few days, will make its bow to the public—a sure sign of growing importance. We can sign claim two dry goods stores, two papers, a fine jewelry establishment, three large hotels, a fine photograph gallery and several of the finest saloons; yet we are sadly in need of many branches of industry. While a rich harvest is waiting here for many to come and harvest it, they are rushing to points already overdone; for instance Tucson and Tombstone.

BUSINESS OPENINGS.

I will give you a list of branches of business badly needed here, and a rich competence will pay those who first come. I don't think any one can charge me with ever making a mistake in my advice, but many have warmly thanked me for giving it. Now what we badly need here is, first: A good tin-smith with tools and stock. If he has not the stock, parties here will advance the money, most of which will be taken out in work. There is at least $500 worth of roofing that could be had now. In lieu of tin, people have to apply shingles. For a good mechanic, sober and industrious, there is no place the equal of this. We also want a good, sober tailor, with goods; none here; nothing but a repairer, and his stitches all go to ruin. A No. 1 painter could find steady employment. We want a good contractor and builder. We want another planning machine. We want a furniture store badly; none here; have to get all our furniture from Chicago or San Francisco, waiting many months for the same. Another large hotel will be ready for furnishing this Fall. A better opening never existed than this. We want a good brewery; ditto a millinery shop; non withing two hundred miles. We want a good blacksmith—one who understands his business. Several good carpenters can get $4 to $5 per day. We want an ice machine; none here. I will guarantee any of the above enterprises to do well here.

SOME INDIAN.

Since my last no more depredations have been committed. We have been promised white troops, who are ordered here, so our prospects for an early settlement of the Indian question are good. One benefit you of California derive is this: all the merchants are ordering goods from San Francisco, or having them sent that way, as there is no security between here and the railroad east.

As this is somewhat lengthy, I will, for the present, say *adios.*

A. S. A.

June 6, 1880.

P.S.—Since writing the above, the stage has come in, bringing the news of a fight between Capt. Parker and his Indian scouts and part of Victorio's band, at a point close to where the late massacre occurred. Parker's scouts ambushed and killed two of Victorio's devils, and wounded another, besides killing five of their horses. Had this not been done, another massacre would no doubt have occurred. Parker and his scouts have made more good Indians in two weeks than

Hatch's command in six months. If Parker had sufficient force he would settle the Indian question in thirty days. The citizens here are going to give him a fine gold watch and chain as an appreciation of his bravery. Of the two Indians killed one is said to be Vic's son, and the other his son-in-law. The scalps are on exhibition here.

In haste,   A. S. A.

←——————→

July 2, 1880, The Evening Express

Correspondence Express

Silver City June 27, 1880

DEAR EXPRESS:—From the many letters and inquiry I am daily receiving from all parts of California, showing your extended circulation and the interest people are taking in New Mexico, I deem it my duty to give some definite information in regard to the same, as it is impossible for me to answer every letter unless I employ a clerk, and as many forget the stamp, they can't expect me to answer. To those who enclose stamps, if I can't answer, I will send one of our weekly papers.

THE HOME OF THE AZTECS.

No doubt exists in my mind, since I have visited the several valleys and caves in this vicinity, where I have found distinct traces of old aqueducts, cemented water ditches, the ruins of the mound-houses, ancient pottery and implements labor that are not used by the Mexicans, immense caves filled with bones, arrows, bows, hatchets of stone, pipes, images of worship covered with hierogly of a tongue unknown at this time, rude devices cut in the walls of monstrous animals unknown to history, that this was the former home of the Aztecs. In the past few weeks many discoveries have been made of immense shafts and tunnels cut through solid stone. The few that have been investigated to any depth or length show well defined ledges of minerals. Some very rich discoveries have lately been made in the Mogollan mountains, some thirty-five miles from here, assays going from $300 to $8,000 per ton. One party refused a quarter of a million dollars for a mine. Within a circuit of forty miles of Silver City there is more mineral wealth than Arizona and Nevada put together possess. I mean what I state, although I will admit my former statements of Tombstone and Patagonia to be true, but right here, in this section of New Mexico, will be shown the wonder of the world so far at mineral wealth is concerned. Right here, adjoining the city limits, a body of ore was discovered in the mine known as the Seventy-Six, showing horn silver and bromide of silver assays $33,000 per ton. Several tons lay in the mine, waiting for the steam hoisting works, and a still larger body is in sight undisturbed. Half a million will not buy this mine. The Cosette mine, that sold a few weeks since for $50,000 is turning out silver bricks by the cart load. The three mills that are running night and day are yielding untold thousands; but because these is no stock for sale the fact is not heralded to the world. Beside those above mentioned, there are many other rich mines being worked. What we need is a forty-stamp mill that will do custom work. A mill for this purpose would pay a large dividend.

CHEAPNESS OF WORKING.

Owing to the abundance of timber and plenty of water, there is no place in my knowledge where ore can be worked so cheap as here. Wood can be bought for $2.50 per cord; water in abundance by digging 30 to 40 feet, and as we don't expect to be cursed by a railroad running through our city, as they can't come nearer than thirty miles, we are bound to be a prosperous place. Again people are coming daily, and as we will in the future have protection, as Gen. Buell is ordered here with fifteen companies of white troops, that will patrol all the roads coming here, all will be safe in traveling hereafter, and I will state once for all, here is the place for men of grit to come to make money, but a poor place for drones. Of the sporting fraternity we have enough. Dance-houses and "such like" are numerous as in all prosperous camps; but there appears to be a ...

MORAL DELIRIUM TREMENS.

That affects all prosperous camps. The first thing a miner thinks of after selling his mine is a glorious jamboree, that all his acquaintances must assist in or get his displeasure.

OUR CLIMATE.

As I have formerly left out this subject, until I could speak from experience, I can truthfully say that we have the most delightful climate I have ever found. At no time has the heat reached 90° generally from 72° to 85° in the middle of the day; at night, 55° to 65°. You always want a pair of blankets at night. Glorious mountain breezes all day. This is the Italy of the Northern Continent, while the poor heathens of Tucson are sweltering in a heat ranging from 100° to 117°. Poor benighted souls, how I pity them! And we are not starving either. Poor souls, 'tis hard to die, isn't it! Never mind I will promise you a pleasant obituary; so let the fiesta go on.

Hastily yours,   A. S. A.

July 16, 1880, The Evening Express

NEW MEXICO

Her New Greatness. Mineral Wealth. The Centre of Mining Interests.
Uncle Sam's White Boys in Blue.

[Special Correspondent Epées]

Silver City, July 11

DEAR EXPRESS:—As your many readers continue to flood me with letters of inquiry about this land of promise and fact, I will revenge myself by using you as a medium of reply. I am daily in receipt of letters from doctors, lawyers, editors, and members of various other professions and trades some even charging me with destroying their peace of mind. If I could, I would send them a plaster to bind up the wound. As I have, with the assistance of others, been "Hatching" for the last thee months, we have accomplished the wonderful feat of turning black into white. In other words, the "Buffalo" troops are being replaced by white ones. Fen. Hatch has been promoted (?) to another field of labor. May the ghosts of those three hundred murdered victims, all blamable to his incompetency haunt his pillow nightly! May the groans of the poor women and children who were burned and mutilated forever ring in his ears! As my poetic friend said, "May the hearth-stove of hell be his pillow."

THE GREAT BOOM REVIVING.

As the undeniable truth of the mineral wealth of Grant County is becoming more generally known, capitalists are again flocking here. Even the fear of Victorio's return will not keep them away. But, as we have now a General in whom we have confidence and who is pursuing a sizeable plan of action, we no longer fear the red devils. The roads are now being patrolled daily from Messilia on the north to Shakespeare south, so that all travel is perfectly secure.

GRANT COUNTY, NEW MEXICO

Of which Silver City is the business centre, is providing to be one of the richest in the Union, although comparatively not prospected at all. The county ranks No. 1 in mineral wealth; no better place in the world for the intelligent prospector or minor than here. We have the Mogollons forty miles north; the Mimbres District; a rich belt twenty-five miles east; Lone Mountains, seven miles west; Clifton and Gold Camp, seventy-five miles south—all depending on this place for supplies, as no other point is accessible; while, right at our doors we have many mines that assay from $60 to $30,000. Pinos Altos, a rich gold camp, is about seven miles north,

166

tributary also to this place, while also the valleys surrounding have some of the finest grazing lands in the world.

SCAN MAG.

While writing the above I heard the clatter of domestic war, and, as a good reporter should, so, I rushed out to investigate. Coming to the scene of action, I found the wife of one of our lawyers on the war path. Having long suspected her liege lord of infidelity, this peaceful Sabbath evening she followed him to the dusky siren's den. In her just wrath she burst in the locked door, when the guilty disciple of Blackstone retreated to the hills with him inamorata. His wife commenced the work of demolition, and what a wreck was there my countrymen! Tar and feathers are strongly talked of, and I presume there will be a vacancy in the legal profession.

THE FOURTH OF JULY.

At no time since my earliest boyhood have I ever seen the Fourth so neglected as here. Not a flag fluttered to the breeze; not a fire-cracker; not even a decent drunk. It appeared as if all were mourning for our butchered dead; no heart to celebrate the birth of the nation which forgets to protect her citizens from the bloody-handed murderous savage.

Yours, A. S. A.

General Don Carlos Buell

August 28 1880, Evening Express

NEW MEXICO

New Mining Discoveries—Weather—Victorio—His Reservation—
A Job Behind the Scenes—Why the War was Brought About.

SILVER CITY, Aug. 22, 1880

Editor Express:—Our mining interests are still progressing, the different mills still adding their quota of silver to the supply of an overburdened country. Poor country! Why don't it divide? New and rich discoveries are of weekly occurrence—now in Eureka district, next in Tres Hermanos, Gold Camp and Mogollons—all sending their rich treasures to inflame our eyes. Truly this is a load of boundless wealth. Old tunnels and shafts are being found, which must have been worked either by the Spaniards in early days of Solomon to get the silver for his temple. Still enough is left to build thousands of temples. All we want is mills to work the ore, and I truly think enough silver and gold can be taken out here to glut the world.

THE WEATHER.

For this last two months has been productive of nothing but rain. It don't simply rain, it literally pours. Washouts east, washouts west; railroads demoralized, miles of track washed away. If every season is like this the railroads will find it more expensive to keep their track in order than the Central Pacific does by reason of its snow difficulties, but as the companies make it up on the tariff, the dear people have to pay for it in the long run. We of this benighted land pay dearly for our few advantages. Not one-half of the articles required for daily use can be had. Those that are kept are at the Dutchman's one per cent. Why don't some of your live California merchants come out here? They could get rich in a few years and then go back and buy one of your fine orange groves and live like princes. I see that Tucson people are jealous of you and warn the people about getting bit in buying property there. Poor, old adobe Tucson! May your shadow never grow less.

VICTORIO

This wary old Chief was driven off his reservation by the drunken act of one of Hatch's officers, named Merrit, who, without cause or provocation, shot at him and his Indians. Old Vic swore revenge and how truly he has kept his word, the hundreds of innocent people he has slain attest. And the commencement of the end is not yet. After a year's fighting, and the reported hundreds of braves that Hatch says were killed (no proof of which can be had), Vic's band from thirty-four has now increased, according to the best reports, to over 500 strong. Oh, what a tale of death will soon be heralded to this world! Vic is but playing with the troops now on the Rio Grande. Soon, like a meteor, he will flash through New Mexico and Arizona, leaving a trail of blood behind. Who is to blame for this? No one but Hatch. Several times when Victorio had only thirty-five or forty Indians with him Hatch could have captured him but did not; and more, it seems as if he did not want to do so. Now, while we have plenty of troops, it seems they are still hampered by his orders. Gen. Buell, if let alone, would no doubt get the best of it, as he is a good and brave officer, and well supported. But red tape and imbecile rules are too much for him.

VICTORIO'S RESERVATIONS.

Where he was and asked to be left to live in peace, is known as the Ojo Caliente country, a reservation thirteen miles square, near the Mexican line, one of the finest spots on earth—a principality, as it were, in the sierras—a valley of beauty surrounded on all sides by mountains. In the valley are immense hot and cold springs, and you can see the steam from the springs for miles distant. The country abounds in game and rich minerals. Government has spent hundreds of thousands of dollars in building agency houses, schools houses and dwellings. Now what they want to do is simply to get this reservation away from the Indians. They commenced by driving Victorio to desperation and with finality kill or remove the balance of the band. Then the party who wants this place will get a grant, or purchase it from the government. You will find in time that this is the whole cause of the war. Hatch carries with him his prospectors and no doubt knows all about the mineral wealth of the reservation. He and some of his pet satellites want this Arcadian for themselves.   A. S. A.

Sept. 2, 1880, The Evening Express.

A DANCE OF DEATH.

On Friday the 20th ult. the first legal hanging that ever occurred in Grant county, if not in New Mexico (as I can hear of no other) took place. A mulatto, who went by the name of Lewis Gaines, belonging to the 9th Cavalry (Hatch's regiment), brutally killed a comrade at Fort Bayard. He was tried before Judge Bristol (who, by the way, is one of the most upright Judges now on the bench) and was sentenced to be hanged. There was another, Chas. Williams, *alias* Bill Livingstone, *alias* Frank Shelly, said to have been born in Bath County, Ky., who ran away from Kentucky for a crime, went to Colorado, where he was brakeman on a railroad for a while; got into a row at Denver, fled to Texas; joined a band of cattle thieves; got into a fight with some of his companions, killed two; fled to Arizona. Officers followed him to Tucson and Tombstone, when they had found he had gone to Mexico, the haven of murderers. Afterwards Williams re-entered New Mexico near Hillsboro, this county. Here he shot a Mexican who charged him $1 for two meals. Afterwards he killed another Mexican in Hillsboro in a fracas about a woman. He was tried soon after Gaines, found guilty and sentenced to be hanged on the same day that Gaines was.

THE DOUBLE HANGING.

On the 20th a large concourse of people assembled to witness the execution. Rumors of a rescue were rife and Sheriff Whitehill summoned a large posse as a guard. The prisoners were given a chance to speak, and, in a long rambling talk, each said in substance that he had been a bad man. Williams said he had done many crimes that would make the hair on his auditor's heads stand on end. But, notwithstanding all these crimes both of the condemned men had got forgiveness by the assistance of a Catholic Priest and Ministers, and they announced that they were going straight to heaven, and in a few minutes would be looking down on us poor sinners. I think there is a great deal of bosh about this last hour forgiveness and it is a bad doctrine to preach. If there is truth in it, what is the use of living good when you can do as you please and go straight to heaven anyhow? I think the sooner this bubble is explained the better. Well, the hanging was a perfect success, and as it was the Sheriff's first attempt, he is entitled to credit. I hope he will keep the machine well oiled as there are many more here who need the same remedy.

REIGN OF TERROR

In the Gila River section of country, including the San Simon district, during the last six weeks there have been eleven murders. This section is filling up with some of the most desperate characters in the Southwest, many coming from Texas to join them. They are organized in bands to rob and kill, and it is said a band of Vigilantes of 104 have been organized also and they are going to ride around that way. No doubt some hemp will be stretched. I think the roughs will soon find it more healthy in Mexico.

Owing to the rain and ravages of the Indian times are dull here at present. There are many trades and callings now over-stocked in your country which would have a good field here. As your people don't seem to want take a bitter with the sweat. I won't mention what the openings are, but let them come and see.   A. S. A.

Silver City, N. M. Aug. 22, 1880

←——→

Colonel Edward Hatch, 9th U.S. Cavalry Regiment, a Buffalo soldier regiment, African-American troops led by white officers.

September, 28, 1880, The Evening Express,

Mesilla, N.M., Sept. 14, 1880

Dear Express: On the 4th inst. I started for this place; got here safely next day. The pets of Granny Schurz jumped the stage, killing the driver and two passengers. Almost every day since they have amused themselves by chasing the coach.

BUELL'S TROOPS

Have been waiting for two months for supplies so that they can take the field, but through the jealousy of Hatch, they are still unsupplied. Buell has no horses for his cavalry and no pack mules; so he is hampered and can do nothing. Part of two companies of the Fourth went after Victorio, but before relief could get up they were repulsed and had to retreat. The Indian scouts who attacked Vic. got two of their men killed and then retreated. They are useless in a square stand-up fight, and are simply being taught how to fight our troops, as they will ultimately join old Vic. embracing the first good show after being discharged. In the meantime they are laying in plenty of ammunition. I am becoming more satisfied each day that the whole thing is one systematic.

BIG STEAL

This last year requisitions have been made on the Quartermaster's Department for 2,400 cavalry horses, 75 Appaloosas, 200 pack mules and other supplies in proportion, which have been allowed. Now, the facts are, only 200 horses, 15 Appaloosas and about 30 pack mules have been delivered. The balance has been stolen by the Santa Fé ring that gets all the contracts. Of course they don't divide. (?) Gen. Buell wanted to buy supplies here in New Mexico, but no, they had to go through the ring, paying $120 for horses that could have been bought here for $75. Only think of it! Hatch making requisitions for eight horses for each cavalryman! While the Indians are murdering the people, these brave men who rule the Department are

ROBBING UNCLE SAM.

And they blame the Democratic Party for trying to keep down the army! Not one regiment is half full, still all the allowances for a full army is gobbled up by these sharks. I say, abolish the army and let each State and Territory take care of itself. If the Government would divide what it costs to keep up these starched bilks each State could save money

178

and be better protected. If the Territory would offer three hundred dollars per head for Vic's band, in less than thirty days not one would be left. Now, it costs over one million dollars for every savage killed. In this last raid the Indians killed twenty white men between here and Arizona. Next you will hear of his being at the San Carlos agency, where he will get 300 more recruits. Rumors are rife that he is going to take in the Hayes party and hold them for ransom. I hope he will give them a big scare so that they will begin to think there are really Indians out here.

MESILLA.

This town is on the Rio Grande, on flat bottom land—a full-blooded Mexican town, where they chain up hogs, plough with a stick, hitch oxen by the horns, use wooden-wheeled carretas, and all the other devices of three hundred years ago. Mr. Casad, an old Los Angeles man, appears to be the only live man here. He has a flour mill and carries on several other industries; has a fine orchard and vineyard. Grapes and fruit are plentiful, but command good prices, most all kinds selling at the orchards at 5 cts. per pound. The wine is far inferior to California wine. They don't "sabe" how to do it.

THE RIO GRANDE

At this place is a migrating stream, fond of changing its bed. A few years ago it ran some three miles from where it is now. Las year there was no river at all. It dried up. From here your correspondent will go to Las Cruses and the Organ Mountain mines; thence return to Silver—if old Vic don't raise this scalp meanwhile.　　　　As ever, ... A. S. A.

December 6, 1880, The Evening Express

BACK AGAIN

Rio Grande—The Rhine of America—Las Cruces—Organ
Mountain Mines—Improvements at Silver City—Some Needed
Wants—Grant County the Place for Capitalists

SILVER CITY, NOV. 29, 1880

Dear Express:—After spending over two months on the Rio
Grande in company with Captain Parker of Indian fame, I
started Las Cruces Silver City ward, being "heeled" by a
Jewish friend with a bottle of old cognac. We bade *adios* to
Las Cruces, whose air is not redolent with the sweet perfume
of Arabia, having for companions inside the coach two
gentlemen who make their living by fingering painted
cardboard. Our cognac soon melted away. When we got to
the town (?) of Miembres—of many houses and about a dozen
inhabitants—Capt. Parker bought a bottle called whisky. Your
correspondent took one swallow. Ye gods! Molten led was no
comparison. For three hours afterward I saw Indians,

rattlesnakes, scorpions, centipedes, Gila monsters and comets. On our way we saw the

MANY MOUNDS

Victorio had built over his slain to keep his memory green. One mound contains eighteen victims; another ten, and so on. We got to Fort Cummings, where we heard what might have been done if Buell had had about 20,000 more troops and ten months more to get ready. But our Mexican neighbors got the best of Vic., and I will drop the subject, as it has been one of the most sickening farces our Government has been guilty of.

At Cummings we received an addition to our load, of several women and children, so we had to take to the top of the stage, where there was already three ahead. But I managed to get a high-toned seat all to myself, and with the aid of several blankets I turned the seat into a Pullman Palace Car. I curled myself up and tried to woo the fair goddess Sleep by singing, "I am lonely to-night, Love, without you," but she would not woo worth a cent. Soon (I suppose from a sense of sympathy) I had about fifty coyotes joining in the chorus. Parker tried to make me believe they were Indians waiting for my scalp, but the ruse was too shallow, as I did not have any scalp. By the frequent use of that Miembres bottle, the contents of which we insisted on the conductor drinking, we got into Silver ahead of time. Our conductor declared his name to be Shakespeare, and that he was a descendant of the veritable old William, and I think his claim is good, as he used some very poetic words to the mules.

LAS CRUCES

This is an old adobe town, situated on the east bank of the Rio Grande, two and a-half miles from La Mesilla, the other ancient town across the river. The two are a fine pair. The perfume that arises from either after a rain would be attar of roses to a skunk. Each of the towns has about 1,500 inhabitants. With few exceptions I think them the laziest people on the face of the earth. A few sons of Abraham and a couple of industrious Germans have most of the country mortgaged to them, and literally own the country and grow rich on not knowing how to ask enough for their commodities. If you had an American he either keeps a whisky shop, is a gambler, or lives off some Mexican woman to whom he has hitched; but as strangers are flocking in with the railroad there will be great change soon as no better land can be found anywhere for raising grapes or fruit of almost any kind. The Mission grapes raised here is much sweeter than in California, but they don't *sabe* making wine, although you cannot buy a gallon of new wine here for less than a dollar. Grapes sell at four cents per pound, and there is a ready market for all that is offered. How long would it take your vineyardists to become bloated bondholders if they could get such prices? I consider this valley the Rhine of America, and land that can now be bought at from $5 to $20 an acre will quadruple in ten years. The Southern Pacific will soon make a junction with the Atchison, Topeka & Santa Fe somewhere near El Paso, at which point there is sure to be a large city.

THE ORGAN MOUNTAIN MINES

Are about fifteen miles directly East of Las Cruces. They are in a beautiful range of mountains resembling very much in formation a gigantic organ from which the range derives its name. The mine mountain is burrowed on all side with prospect holes each not much larger than a jack-rabbit hole. Each prospector claims a shaft of twelve feet. These mines are all claimed by their owners to be rich, and from specimens that were shown me I can't doubt it, as I recognized carbonates from Leadville, horn silver from the Silver King, some from the Lucky Cuss and other places. Who can doubt that a mountain which yields such a variety of rich ores is a Bonanza? But seriously I do not think there are any mines east of the Rio Grande one fourth as good as claimed. The formation is not there. But, in a few years, this valley will not need mines as her agricultural resources are worth millions, and her manufacturing facilities are unexcelled. All she wants is to kill off her drones and go to work. This valley, like Mexico, is at least two hundred years behind the times. The railroad, the great civilizer and the coming Yank will bring her

184

to the front soon. *Ojala*, mis amigos!

SILVER CITY AND GRANT COUNTY.

Passing the rounds since my return, it seems to me that a magician has visited this ciudad La Plata. New two-story business houses on every street; building still going on and not a vacant house yet. Nearly one hundred new houses have been built this Summer, and not one wooden one—all brick and adobe. We have now a large stove and tin shop, which sold thirty stoves the first three days of the opening. We have a tailor with goods. A large millinery store will open on the first. Another 15-stamp custom quartz mill will be done in sixty days.

WHAT WE NEED BADLY.

A good fruit and family grocery; a hardware store; a brewery, an ice machine. For all of these industries there is a fine opening. Come along some of ye who pant for the almighty dollar.

Our mines are still going ahead. Rich discoveries are of weekly occurrence, and, as I have said before, there is no better locality in the United States than Grant county, New Mexico. Here is a fine opening for mining capitalists, as our mines have not as yet reached the high prices of Arizona mines, although equally as good, if not better.

A. S. A.

January 27, 1881, The Evening Express

A BIG STRIKE AT SILVER CITY

Our Correspondent One of the Lucky Lectors
General News—Bright Prospects of the Camp.

SILVER CITY, Jan. 23 1881.

EDITOR EXPRESS:—Owing to the dearth of anything new until the present week, I have failed to write you, but this last week an enormous deposit of gold has been struck on the borders of the city.

THE OLD TIGER MINE,

That has been worked off and on for several years as a silver mine, was bonded about sixty days since to the Carrolton Mining Co. for $3000. The Company went to work to develop the property, and last week, after reaching a depth of forty-five feet, they struck a small seam of gold bearing quartz, which has widened out to over three feet, bearing free gold. The rock assays from $100 to $5000 per ton. They have now on the dump about forty tons that will yield them at least $100,000. In the adjoining clam, owned by a fortunate wielder of the razor, at a depth of four feet from the top, free gold in quartz was struck yesterday. Your correspondent having timely notice of the first find, located four claims on the same lead. Out of three ounces of decomposed quartz taken out of "The Lucky Joe," one of my locations, pounded up in a mortar, I got from 20 to 30 colors. Everybody here is simply wild over these.

ENORMOUS DEPOSITS.

Claims are being taken up in all directions. As I have ofttimes stated, this will be one of the richest camps in the world. I send you with this a specimen picked off the dump, *not selected.* The company has to keep a guard night and day to keep thieves from stealing the ore. Last Sunday night over a ton was stolen from the dump. As it is just like money lying loose, it proves too tempting for a class that always lies around a mining camp. Two more mills and a system of reduction works are going up, and in a short time we will have a camp of 10,000 in habitants. Good carpenters are in great demand; steady work and good pay awaits them. We have had one regular...

INDIAN MASSACRE,

But as Hatch says the Indians must be caught, that settles it. In about sixty days the two railroads will connect, and there will be only fifty miles of staging from Shakespeare, so the danger then will be comparatively over.

THE WEATHER THIS WINTER,

Is simply delightful. We have had only one slight sprinkle of snow. The temperature is like the months of September and October in Kansas and Missouri. The good people are having fine times with dances, masquerades, and so forth. New-comers are flocking in, and it is an easy matter to get up fifty to sixty couples for a dance. The ladies (God bless them!) have now got a milliner, and loves of hats and fine feathers are visible every day. We are getting quite city-like. We now sport three divines, and so I saw three undeniable devils at the masquerade the other night, I suppose the matter of religion is a stand-off. Hoping before many months to return and buy one of those orange orchards, I am as ever, yours,   A. S. Addis.

June 20, 1881, The Evening Express

Copper Mines.

The Greatest Bonanza on the Continent—Better than Silver or Gold—A Watershed Mineral Belt.

EDITOR EXPRESS:—In my last I promised you a short history of the above mines. Some eight years ago they were discovered by Robert B. Metcalf. Having no capital he tool in the Lisinsky brothers and Freudenthal, making four shares. After a few months these parties wishing to develop, and Metcalf not having the money to invest, sold out to his partners for about $1,000. The Lisinskys then went to work. Being inexperienced in copper mining and having many failures in working the ore, they got involved to the extent of one hundred and seventy thousand dollars. After repeated failures in trying different furnaces and water jackets, they abandoned everything but the simple old Mexican plan, which they have kept going from the start with little improvements in furnaces. I think now that no furnace they are using cost them more than five hundred dollars. Copper, keeping at a low figure (some 8 cents per pound in New York), very little margin was left for profit, but adopting the store system of paying in goods they kept fighting the good fight till copper took a rise to fifteen cents. Then prosperity commenced and, in a very short time, all debts were paid. A railroad to the mines was built to save expense in hauling ore, and in seven years the mines have yielded about four millions of dollars, and the property is probably worth a million and a half more. The output of the mines every day is over 17,000 pounds from one furnace. When they work two this amount is double. There is now at the furnace over ...

FOUR MILLION POUNDS

Of bullion. Transportation can't be got, to keep the dumps clear of bullion, although some eight to ten trains are hauling away bullion with return loads of coke that is brought from Europe to work the furnaces. An immense quantity of goods are also brought in, as probably one thousand people live off this one mine.

This proves what legitimate, honest mining can accomplish. None of your thieving Eastern Stock swindles.

The Company is also now working two more mines and they expect to largely increase their works. In less than a year they will have a branch railroad that will haul away their bullion. The Copper Queen, one of the above mines, now shows better than ever did the Longfellow out of which the four millions was taken. The Colorado mine is fully equal to the Queen. I truly consider this group of copper mines the ...

GREATEST BONANZA,

On the Northern Continent—better than silver or gold, and in less than ten years you will see a city on the San Francisco River that will outvie Virginia in her palmist days. All the ore is easily worked, and at a very low figure the profits are large. As the electric light is now surety, the demand for copper will be quadrupled.

Other rich mines are owned in the immediate vicinity of the above. Metcalf, Porter and Crawford own a group of seven mines for which they ask $1,580,000. A New York firm of capitalists are now negotiating for the same. Other small groups equally as rich are for sale, and I really think that any mie of the lot that is offered for sale will pay for itself in ore now in sight on top of the ground.

FOR CAPITALISTS

I consider this the best field for honest, legitimate mining that can be found. While many are rushing to Mexico where everything is uncertain, paying fancy figures for mines the Spaniards gutted hundreds of years ago, right at home far richer mines can be had for less money and immediate returns, without employing expensive machinery and fancy superintendents. But, somehow, the more humbug and rascality connected with mines the more popular they become, while honest, legitimate property will go a begging. But it's the same old story, of miners leaving $20—per day diggins' to go after some wonderful Gold Lakes or mountains they hear of. I say to capitalists, come out and see this wonderful rich copper region.

Brevity is the soul of wit, but a short article will not do justice to this camp, and if my article is too long sectionize it. These...

IMMENSE COPPER MINES

Lie between the Frisco and Eagle rivers in Graham County, Arizona, adjoining the New Mexican line. These streams run about north and south, and empty into the Gila River, about fifteen miles from Clifton. The Frisco is about as large as the Santa Ana River in San Bernardino County. The eagle is not so large. Along the Frisco for fifteen miles are rich placers, now being got ready for extensive work. Long pipes are being laid four miles for hydraulic work along the west bank of the Frisco. Many rich gold leads have been found, some being worked. Between the Frisco and the Eagle, about half way is the rich copper mountains. Between the copper mines and the Eagle river is galena and silver. So here is a space of eight miles we have the wonderful combination of

194

gold placers, gold veins, copper mines, lead mines, silver mines, and hot springs, that *never failing indicator* of rich mines.

NOW WHERE ON EARTH...

can you find the equal to this region? Certainly not in Mexico, which people are going wild over. I have been all over there and I know nothing in that country which equals the eight miles of territory I speak of. Here capital can be safely invested that will pay with honest management, 100 per cent per annum. New, ye seekers for fortunes, come out and see this section, and after you give it an honest and fair investigation, if you don't agree with men, I will quit writing. Don't get infatuated with Mexico before you know your own country. Don't put your money in gopher holes or old worked-out mines when you can come here and see in sight on top of the ground enough tp pay you all the capital you will put in without risking what you can't see. Next week I go to Georgetown, another place where honest mining is done. No stock on the market.

As ever, A. S. A.

SILVER CITY, June 14, 1881.

Supplemental.

———————

Silver City, June 14, 81 }
 5 P. M.   }
 just received a private dispatch from New York, which capitalists of that city have purchased the Lisinsky property, consisting of the Longfellow, Copper Queen and King, for the sum of two million dollars. So, you see I did not make a mistake in my valuation of the property.

A. S. A.

←———→

Alfred Shea Addis

Born January 25, 1831
Phiadelphia, Pennsylania

Died September 10, 1886
El Paso, Texas